D0861572

ARROWHEADS &
STONE ARTIFACTS

Illustration 1 Petrikin's Hill arrowhead, Greeley, Colorado.

ARROWHEADS & STONE ARTIFACTS

A PRACTICAL GUIDE FOR THE AMATEUR
ARCHAEOLOGIST

SECOND EDITION

C. G. YEAGER

PRUETT PUBLISHING COMPANY
BOULDER, COLORADO

Library of Congress Cataloging-in-Publication data

Yeager, C. G. (Carl Gary), 1942–
    Arrowheads & stone artifacts : a practical guide for the amateur
archaeologist / C. G. Yeager.—2nd ed.
      p. cm.
    Includes bibliographical references (p.) and index.
    ISBN 0-087108-912-2
    1. Archaeology—Field work. 2. Arrowheads—Collectors and collecting.
3. Stone implements—Collectors and collecting. I. Title: Arrowheads and
stone artifacts. II. Title.

CC76.Y43 2000
930.1—dc21
                                   00-036607

All illustrations and photographs by the author unless otherwise credited, with the following exceptions: illustrations 1, 16, 21, 36, 75, 101, 126, 133, 134, 146 by Norman Wood; cover photograph and illustrations 13, 14, 15, 16, 17, 18, 19, 20, 21 by Stephen Collector; illustration 151 by Allen R. Crawford; illustration 152 by Sue Yeager; illustration 153 by Katie DeLeo.

Printed in the United States
09 08 07 06 05 04 03 02   5 4 3

Cover design by Julie Noyes Long

*This book is dedicated to my wife, Sue, who has been my steady com-
panion in hunting artifacts for many years. A husband could never ask
for a more faithful and devoted wife—she is a real trooper. She has always provided faith and inspiration when the going gets tough. When
hunting for artifacts she is usually the first one out and the last one in,
no matter how the hunting is or what the conditions are like. Her energy
is not directed toward being the first one to find all the artifacts—she
genuinely enjoys watching others find nice artifacts, too. She is very generous, compassionate, and truly a lot of fun to hunt artifacts with.*

Illustration 2   Sue Yeager at homestead site in central Wyoming.

CONTENTS

LIST OF ILLUSTRATIONS

Illustration 3   The home of J. M. B. Petrikin on "Petrikin's Hill" in Greeley, Colorado, as it looked in 1950. Note the native sod in the area of the prehistoric campsite. This site is now occupied by the student center of the University of Northern Colorado. Photo courtesy of the Greeley Municipal Museum.

FOREWORD

Anyone who frequents the great outdoors stands a good chance of encountering artifactual evidence of earlier inhabitants. Such an experience can affect individuals in different ways. At the age of four, while trailing along horseback behind a herd of cattle on the family ranch in Wyoming, I noticed a strange appearing stone. Not knowing what it was, I put it in my pocket and that evening my grandmother identified it as the most unusual artifact she had ever seen. From that day on, I was hooked on archaeology and went through all of the stages of collecting and finally, realizing that archaeology was more than gathering artifacts, decided to pursue the subject through the academic discipline of anthropology, a decision I have never regretted.

The other extreme is exemplified by an old sheepherder I knew who would pick up artifacts, lay each one on a flat rock and smash it with another rock, and then throw the pieces as far as he could. This all changed on the day he discovered he could trade a complete projectile point for a drink at the local bar in town. One result of this was displays of artifacts glued to boards with no record of provenience and little if any archaeological value.

Between these two extremes lies a large group that, from a wide variety of experiences, have become hooked on archaeology as an avocation. They occupy many different walks of life and a good share of their spare time is occupied in the pursuit of artifacts and learning more about them. Most of these individuals read the relevant literature, are serious in making worthwhile contributions to archaeology, and maintain a good level of cooperation with professional archaeologists. Collectively, avocationals have shared information that has led to the identification and study of sites that provide a large share of the present data, particularly in the area of Paleoindian studies where sites are often small and the forces of nature rapidly expose and destroy evidence. We need the practiced eyes of knowledgeable avocationals who can spot this kind of evidence and bring it to the attention of researchers.

In the 1986 edition of this book, the late Dr. H. Marie Wormington, that venerable First Lady of North American Paleoindian studies, clearly stated the obligations imposed avocational archaeologists. (1) Keep accurate records of what you find. (2) Maintain contacts with researcher so that an important site or other forms of data will not slip through the cracks. (3) Educate yourself so that you can intelligently discuss and transmit the results of your findings to others.

Things have changed for avocationals in the last few decades. Collecting on Federal and state lands is severely restricted and, as a group, private landowners are more deeply and rightfully concerned about the liabilities that can develop through trespassing, During this same time period, the methodology of archaeology has changed radically placing a much greater onus on the avocationals to keep abreast of new developments. However, this revised edition offers the serious avocationals a directive for pursuing an interest and at the same time contributing in positive ways to the scientific descriptions of archaeology.

GEORGE C. FRISON
Professor Emeritus
University of Wyoming

PREFACE

After fourteen years and excellent sales of the first edition of this book, it has become obvious to me that I have learned a lot since 1986 and that this book should be updated, expanded, and, in some cases, corrected. As I stated in the original edition, I do not claim to be an expert in the field of archaeology. I have, however, continued to study and have associated myself with a number of individuals who are far more knowledgeable than I am. Through this study and collaboration comes this revised edition, a practical guide for the amateur collector of arrowheads and stone artifacts that provides guidance on how to collect properly.

As the old saying goes, we never stop learning. Through self-education, reading, and continued study, a person can't help but learn more over a period of fourteen years. Also, as time passes, social attitudes change, and, as we all know, things that were accepted in the past or taken for granted may now be frowned upon or be controversial. Likewise, I now have a different attitude about some things as opposed to how I felt fourteen years ago. All in all, then, change is in order for this publication if it is to continue to educate and inform those avocationalists who are interested in archaeology. A reader of this book in the new millennium should not be presented with outdated ideas from "way back in the 1900s"!

I have, therefore, attempted to improve upon this book by introducing the reader to some of those people who have educated me over the years and who have supported my efforts in revising this publication (see acknowledgments). Because of increased sensitivity in our society, I feel that first and foremost, a code of ethics of artifact hunting should be set forth, and this I have done at the beginning of the revision. In this regard, I have also included a separate chapter on what are generally referred to as "antiquity laws." Many new laws and regulations have been passed by Congress, administrative agencies of the federal government, and state and local governments that affect amateur archaeologists. I have not set forth my interpretation of these laws as the legal advice of a lawyer, but simply my own opinion of them. I do not intend to create an attorney-client relationship with anyone who reads this book.

Next, I have included a new chapter, Why Look for Artifacts? Here I explain not only why I hunt artifacts, but why many others do, too. Hunting of arrowheads and stone artifacts is a wholesome and worthwhile endeavor and is not necessarily a destructive and disrespectful activity.

Chapter 6 has been revised and retitled, Arrowhead, Spearpoint, or Knife? What I once assumed was an arrowhead may have, in fact, been used as a spearpoint or knife. Likewise, what I once referred to as a spearpoint, primarily because of its size, may have actually been a stone knife. This chapter will help alleviate some of the confusion.

Since a substantial number of arrowheads—and other stone tools, for that matter—have been reworked, sharpened, or reshaped, I have now included a new section on this topic in chapter 6. Many people, myself included, have often wondered why a projectile point or tool appears to be poorly made or out of proportion. Reworking, of course, is the obvious answer to this question.

Today, a large number of nice artifacts are being found in riverbeds or creek beds. I have revised chapter 8 to include this type of site among the other types previously set forth in the original edition of this book.

Since "arrowhead hunting" can lead to many other fascinating and interesting discoveries, I have expanded chapter 9 on such incidental finds and have also included more information on pottery.

Chapter 10 has been included because my ideas on modern-day flintknapping have changed somewhat over the years. I once frowned on today's flintknapping, but I have now discovered that it can be a useful tool in understanding archaeology. Professional archaeologists have frequently used modern-day flintknapping for valuable information in their study of lithic technology.

I have added more precise information on cataloging and documenting a personal collection in chapter 11, and in chapter 12 I have included more information on amateur archaeological organizations and their activities.

In summary, every chapter of the first edition of this book has been revised, some to a greater extent than others, and six new chapters have been added. A glossary of archaeological terms and a recommended reading list have also been added. My hope is that these changes yield meaningful additional content for the reader. The study of archaeology continues to change as new advanced research techniques are developed, so there is, no doubt, a strong likelihood that this book may need to be revised again.

ACKNOWLEDGMENTS

As is usual when writing a book such as this, it would be impossible to name everyone who contributed. At the same time, I am obligated to identify certain contributors who were essential to the production of the book. I should begin with the farmers, ranchers, and landowners who make the hunting of artifacts possible through their kindness and generosity.

More specifically, my appreciation goes to the Municipal Museum of Greeley, Colorado, in providing the photograph of the Petrikin home in Greeley. My appreciation also goes to The Stackpole Company of Harrisburg, Pennsylvania, for their permission to reproduce illustrations 23, 25, 26, 27, and 28. These well-drawn illustrations were originally found in *The Beginner's Guide to Archaeology* authored by Louis A. Brennan.

I would like to sincerely thank Jerry Keenan, formerly of Pruett Publishing Company, who had faith in me and confidence in this book right from the beginning in the early 1980s. Jerry was very cooperative and easy to work with, just as Jim Pruett, of Pruett Publishing Company, is today. Jim's encouragement and suggestions, including the addition of the glossary, have been valuable to the revision. Allen and Jean Crawford, perhaps unknowingly to them, steered me in the right direction with my archaeological pursuits years ago and should have been mentioned in the original edition of this publication. Allen and Jean played a major role in the early 1980s in the "rebirth" of the Loveland Stone Age Fair and its primary sponsor, The Loveland Archaeological Society, Inc., a Colorado nonprofit organization. Many other members of this group, both past and present, have, likewise, perhaps unknowingly, contributed greatly to my overall knowledge of archaeology. I hesitate to name individuals because I will omit several who should be mentioned. I simply have to mention, however, Garry Weinmeister, George Stewart, and Ray Lambert. I am convinced that these three people know as much about archaeology as anyone I know who has never had formal training. Their knowledge of archaeology is really quite remarkable. In addition, George Stewart, who is an excellent flintknapper, made the contemporary items shown in illustrations 32 and 74. Garry Weinmeister likewise graciously consented to my photography of his artifacts shown in illustration 109. I would also like to thank Jean Steinhoff, longtime secretary of The Loveland Archaeological Society, Inc., whom I worked with several years ago in developing the code of ethics included in this revised edition.

I have been associated with the Loveland Stone Age Fair for almost twenty years and have had the opportunity to work with a number of professional archaeologists who have spoken at the fair, including such noted archaeologists as Dr. George Frison of the University of Wyoming and Dr. Dennis Stanford of the Smithsonian Institution. I have learned much from their presentations and many publications. I have also learned a lot from many of the amateur archaeologists who have participated in this annual event. There are too many to acknowledge, but I simply have to mention the late Bert Mountain, Ed Gregory, and Homer McGeorge. These kind individuals have shared their vast knowledge with me on many occasions over the years, which I appreciate very much.

I also want to thank my sister, Carolyn Millspaugh, for providing the Petrikin's Hill arrowhead that was photographed for the frontispiece. My appreciation goes also to Judy Wood for providing me with the artifact photographed in illustration 36. Likewise, I would like to thank Judy's husband, Norman Wood, who did an excellent job with some of the photography found in the book. My longtime secretary, Dorothy Manning, was very helpful in typing and proofreading the revised manuscript. She was also generous in loaning me artifacts found in Wyoming by her father, Frank Wilkinson, which are the subjects of several of the illustrations herein. Some of my antiquity law materials were assembled and provided to me by my longtime friend Bruce Bergstrom, whom I sincerely thank for his contribution. Bruce saved me considerable time and effort in my legal research. I would also like to express my appreciation to good friends Vince and Carol Sanchez, for generously hosting my wife and me at their ranch in New Mexico on more than one occasion. They kindly allowed me to photograph the site shown in illustration 97. Another longtime friend, Steve Goodroad, was quite generous in giving me the artifacts shown in illustrations 99 and 100. I would also like to express my sincere appreciation to Dr. George Frison for taking the time out of a busy schedule to write the kind and thoughtful foreword for this revised edition.

Last but not least, I want to thank my entire family for the good times we have had on the many camping and artifact-hunting trips we have taken over the years. Those precious moments with my grand-daughters, watching them grow up and learn about nature and prehis-toric times, will never be forgotten. My wife, Sue; our daughter, Debbie DeLeo; and her husband, Ted, also found many of the artifacts photographed herein. Sue was also very helpful during the revision by supplying advice, encouragement, and assistance in typing. Finally, the presence of my granddaughters, Nicole, Katie, and Megan, have made all of my efforts worthwhile from start to finish.

INTRODUCTION

A lifelong hobby began for me by accident almost fifty years ago on a hill on the edge of Greeley, Colorado. This hill, formerly known as Petrikin's Hill, was then owned and occupied by the late J. M. B. Petrikin, prominent Greeley banker, and was actually rural property located on the edge of town near a farm owned by Mr. Petrikin. The hill itself was the highest point in the immediate vicinity, and many years ago, with the absence of trees, there was, no doubt, a beautiful, panoramic view of the Cache la Poudre River valley to the north and the South Platte River valley to the south and east.

As kids, my sister and I used to play on the hill with Mr. Petrikin's permission. One day, quite unexpectedly, my sister found a perfect arrowhead not too far south of Mr. Petrikin's home on an area of native soil left undisturbed, which probably looked the same as it did hundreds of years ago. Even though we were very young, we recognized the significance of what my sister had found, and the excitement I felt then is hard to describe. My curiosity got the best of me, and it wasn't long until I was visiting with Mr. Petrikin about the arrowhead. I found out that many arrowheads had been found in the past when a basement was dug under Mr. Petrikin's home on top of the hill. Mr. Petrikin explained

Illustration 4 The author's Folsom point, found south of Yuma, Colorado, in 1958, with only a small portion of the base missing. The Folsom is one of the oldest points and is not often found in many private collections.

to me that many years ago, an ancient prehistoric camp was located on the top of the hill, right where I stood talking to him. From that day on my interest in archaeology grew steadily—all resulting from that one small arrowhead. That arrowhead, still cherished by my sister, is featured on the frontispiece of this book. Petrikin's Hill is now occupied by the student center of the University of Northern Colorado, and no trace whatsoever of its original inhabitants or the ancient campsite remains.

Illustration 5 Campsite located at the author's home, west of Loveland, Colorado. The site is situated on an east slope and lies below a spring located to the left and below the saddle in the ridge.

My thirst for knowledge of stone artifacts has been unquenchable since those early days. A grade school field trip on the South Platte River near Evans, Colorado, led to the discovery of another stone artifact, which again was found quite by accident. Later on, my grandfather, Earl Worden, took me to a ridge west of Loveland, Colorado, that is now occupied by a subdivision. There I finally found my first actual arrowhead. A few years later, shortly after I began to drive, a visit with relatives in Yuma, Colorado, led to a side trip where I found a beautiful spearpoint that I later discovered was a true Folsom point. This Folsom point, which is now framed, is shown in illustration 4. In the same area, I found five other arrowheads—all in less than ten minutes. This still stands as a personal record.

After several years of hunting artifacts in both Colorado and Wyoming, I made my home west of Loveland, Colorado, where my biggest surprise was yet to come. One day while working in my garden,

I found part of a white arrowhead. Further searching in the area led to the discovery of other flint materials and arrowheads, and, as it turned out, my acreage contained a prehistoric campsite, as shown in illustration 5. Like so many others, this campsite is located just below a break in a ridge and next to a spring. It wasn't long until my wife and daughter became interested in the artifacts that I had hunted for years. As the months passed, artifact hunting became an interesting and very worthwhile family hobby—something that has grown steadily over the years and probably will continue to do so in the future.

In writing and revising this book, my approach has been to present stone-artifact hunting as both a learning experience and as an individual or family activity. I have not written this book claiming to be an archaeological expert but have merely tried to present a practical guide for the amateur collector so that he or she will have a better idea of what to do and how to search and collect properly. As with any other endeavor, there is both a right way and a wrong way to pursue the desired goal, as you will see in the pages that follow.

I would hope that this book might bring professional and amateur archaeologists into closer harmony and cooperation as they pursue a common goal—the discovery and study of artifacts and the cultures from which they came.

CHAPTER 1

AMATEUR ARCHAEOLOGISTS' CODE OF ETHICS

Strict adherence to the following code of ethics will result in an individual being a responsible and courteous amateur archaeologist who should gain the respect of professional archaeologists and the general public:

ALWAYS OBTAIN PERMISSION

Always obtain permission from the proper landowner before embarking on a field trip. Most landowners are quite receptive if a person will simply ask rather than trespass. In some cases, you can safely obtain permission from a person who is simply leasing land. The preferred approach, however, is to get permission from both the lessee and the owner of the property. When hunting a riverbed, be careful to obtain permission from the adjoining landowners on both sides of the river or creek. Some state laws require a person to carry written permission from the landowner at all times. (See chapter 2 for further discussion on the legality of your planned activity.)

INFORM AND COMMUNICATE

Inform the person from whom you obtain permission exactly what you plan to do, where you plan to go, and when you plan to arrive and leave the property. It is also a good idea to describe the vehicle you will drive and who will be with you. Communicate that you only drive on established roads, that you leave gates as you find them, that you don't carry a gun, and that you won't bring your dog with you. Such positive communication lays a good foundation for your hunting activity, both at the moment and hopefully on future visits.

ONLY SURFACE HUNT ON PRIVATELY OWNED LAND

Only surface hunt on privately owned land, and *never* search for or remove artifacts from any federal, state, or locally owned government land. There should be absolutely no exceptions, even if you have a good friend who happens to be employed by a governmental body. Government employees should set a good example and not engage in this activity as well. The risks are simply too great and the punishment potentially too severe to hunt on any land that is not privately owned. (Also see chapter 2 regarding the legality of this type of activity.)

RESPECT THE LAND AND OTHER PRIVATE PROPERTY

When hunting for arrowheads and stone artifacts, treat others' property like you would want someone to treat yours. For instance, gates should always be left the way you find them. A lot of ranchers leave gates between pastures open so that livestock can pass freely from one pasture to another. In the absence of livestock, sometimes a rancher will leave gates open to facilitate passing through the area. Livestock and crops or vegetation should always be respected. Animals should not be disturbed, and driving should be limited to established roads only. Trash and litter should not be scattered, and smoking should only be done inside vehicles, the disposal of cigarettes limited to the ashtrays inside the car. In this day and age, many people do not want cigarette butts extinguished on their property. In fact, a fire can start very easily in dry vegetation. Because of this, when camping, campfires should not be used during these times, even if you have permission.

It is also a good idea to never carry a gun for any reason, nor to take a dog along. For obvious reasons, the presence of a gun tends to create understandable apprehension on the part of a landowner, and especially a farmer or rancher. There is simply no reason to carry a gun while hunting artifacts. A small pocketknife is about the only "weapon" that could ever be necessary. Dogs can very easily stir up and chase livestock. Such activity can certainly lessen the chances of any return visits in the future. Furthermore, unless the landowner is a relative or extremely close friend, motorcycles and all-terrain vehicles should not be used. These vehicles can disturb livestock and destroy vegetation off established roadways.

REPORT NOTEWORTHY OR UNUSUAL ARCHAEOLOGICAL SITES

Report noteworthy finds to the professional archaeological community, *but only with the landowner's consent.* Some landowners may have valid reasons why they would not want their property to be the focus of an archaeological project. However, reporting sites is one way the amateur can contribute significantly to the valuable study of archaeology by the professional community. It is, without a doubt, a very good way to gain the respect of professional archaeologists. Some will readily admit that amateurs have reported as many as three-fourths of the major sites that have been investigated and contributed valuable scientific knowledge.

BE HUMBLE AND APPRECIATIVE

Not many of us own enough land to have our own private hunting ground, and most of us are at the mercy of the private landowner in our endeavor to look for artifacts. We should, therefore, acknowledge this and be thankful and appreciative for this privilege. We should always thank those who have given us permission—not only in person, but also with a thank-you letter after we have returned home. If you can return a favor to a landowner in any way, always seriously consider doing so. I have, for instance, given many of my pastel artworks to farmers and ranchers as a small token of my appreciation for their generosity and hospitality. Likewise, I have reported sick livestock to ranchers and other unusual situations I have observed. Furthermore, I take a personal interest in the landowners and their lives, too—I am not only interested in what archaeological treasures I can find on their property.

NEVER DIG OR EXCAVATE

Never dig or excavate on private property, even if you have permission to do so. Valuable scientific information can be lost forever with irresponsible excavation, even by a well-meaning individual who shovels up an archaeological site on his or her own land. This should be left to professional archaeologists who know what they are doing. In recent years especially, irresponsible individuals have literally destroyed archaeological sites, in some cases through the use of bulldozers. Needless to say, a vast amount of archaeological knowledge can be lost forever with careless digging, and amateur excavation is the main thing that disturbs the professional community and general public. Simply put, archaeological sites should be preserved for professional investigation and evaluation. We owe to those that follow us to preserve such sites. None of us like or appreciate the label of "pot hunter," and the vast majority of us are not. Let's keep it that way and gain the respect of anyone who might tend to be critical of our activities. Artifact hunting should be neither a compulsive nor a destructive activity.

CATALOG AND DOCUMENT

Catalog and document what you find, where you found it, when you found it, and any other noteworthy facts and circumstances. One thing that professional archaeologists criticize is the failure of many amateurs to keep adequate records and label artifacts efficiently. If you catalog and document your collection, you will never be sorry, because as the years go by and the number of artifacts increases, it is impossible to remember where everything was found. (For more information, see chapter 11.)

CONTINUE TO EDUCATE YOURSELF

Arrowhead hunting can actually be easier when you are better informed and educated in the scientific and practical aspects of archaeology. Today there is a vast amount of published material readily available to the average person, including information on the Internet. A person hunting arrowheads and stone artifacts should not just be excited about a nice find, but should also be aware of its archaeological significance.

RESPECT THE FEELINGS AND OPINIONS OF OTHERS

Respect not only those with whom you are hunting, but also other archaeological contacts and acquaintances. When hunting with others, do not expect to find all the artifacts; enjoy the opportunity to observe the discovery of a nice artifact by someone else. Observing this conduct will protect friendships and ensure that you won't have to hunt for artifacts alone. Common courtesy is a good rule of thumb to observe in all aspects of hunting arrowheads and stone artifacts.

CHAPTER 2

ΛΝΤΙQUITY LΛWS–IS YOUR ΛCTIVITY LEGΛL?

Some legal authorities have commented that the one certain thing about the law is that it always changes. As an attorney, this is one of the main things that has always frustrated me in the practice of law. The following information is not meant to create an attorney-client relationship with anyone who reads this book. It is meant to simply inform readers that in this day and age, one has to be *very* careful with any activity involved with arrowhead hunting, especially activities in the field.

There was a time several years ago, under the old federal Antiquities Law of 1906, that people really didn't have to worry too much about where they surface hunted artifacts as long as they had permission and were not hunting in a national park, national monument, or other specially designated government area (such as a military base, etc.), and as long as their activity involved *no* excavation or digging. Historically, the laws of treasure trove were based on the principle that lost or abandoned personal property belonged to the person upon whose land the items were found. In other words, the farmer or rancher had first claim to treasure trove found upon the land they owned. Naturally, he or she could give permission to someone who wanted to search for such items, and when found, such items presumptively belonged to the person who found them. If a person found such items without permission, then, arguably, he or she could be found guilty of theft and trespassing. When you stop to think about it, this really does make sense. If you were spading up your garden and found an old coin, wouldn't you feel that the coin should belong to you? I would suspect that most people would feel this way. Years ago, when it came to government land, I believe the thinking then was that such items of treasure trove, when found on the surface of government-owned land in general (excluding, again, national parks, national monuments, and similar specially designated areas or sites), belonged to the "public," with *public* generally defined as including you and I—when you or I found such item, then, because we were a member of the public, it was ours to keep. Nowadays, of course, under current antiquities laws, *public* is in essence defined as "the government," and such items now belong to the government, which, technically speaking, does not include you or me. Hopefully, you get the point, and in my opinion, this is the basic theory behind most modern-day antiquities laws. Under some current state or federal laws, legislative bodies (and the courts, in interpreting such laws) have now attempted to redefine the historical laws of treasure trove. In some instances, the argument is now that all items of treasure trove, no matter where they are found, belong to the public, with *the public* being defined as the government. It could easily be argued that this is going too far—but, naturally, this would be my opinion as an arrowhead hunter. The end result of this philosophy, of course, would be that any hunting and removal of any treasure trove, including the example of the old coin in the garden, or, of course, any stone artifact, would be totally illegal because such items all belong to the government. In other words, we are, in effect, stealing from the government under such a theory.

For many years, the federal government and most, if not all, state governments have had laws protecting grave sites, and rightly so. Grave sites should be protected whether they are located within an established cemetery or whether they are historical or prehistorical graves located at random throughout the land. To me, there is just something fundamentally offensive about digging or destroying a grave site. This, I feel, was probably the true basis of the federal Antiquities Act of 1906. Congress was primarily concerned with excavation of federal land, which, in most instances up until that time, probably involved grave sites and treasure trove. Also, it can logically be argued that "treasure trove," when found in a grave, is not lost or abandoned property, and is therefore not true treasure trove. Such items were probably not truly lost or abandoned, but were put there for valid religious or ceremonial purposes.

In 1906, then, surface hunting and removal of stone artifacts was generally not frowned upon. Under the Archaeological Resource Protection Act of 1979 (ARPA), however, such activity is now not only frowned upon, but declared to be illegal under all the federal regulations promulgated by federal agencies pursuant to the provisions of ARPA. ARPA gave these agencies the authority to adopt regulations in order to carry out the provisions of ARPA. These regulations are found in the Code of Federal Regulations (CFR) and have been promulgated by such agencies as the Bureau of Land Management (BLM) and National Forest Service (NFS). These adopted Federal Regulations seem to go further in their restrictions than what is set forth in ARPA itself. The end result, however, is clear—a person cannot legally hunt and remove any artifacts, including stone artifacts, from *any* federal land. Also, most, if not all, state governments have similar laws in force nowadays, and *no* hunting or removal of any artifacts, including stone artifacts, should be done on *any* state land, either. This is why I have set forth in my code of ethics (see chapter 1) that arrowhead hunting should only be done on private land with proper permission. Special caution should be taken in hunting riverbeds, lakeshores, and seashores because these areas are often owned by federal, state, and local governments, and removal of artifacts from these places is illegal. Always make sure you are hunting on privately owned land, and when hunting a riverbed, obtain permission from all adjoining landowners on both sides of the river.

I have currently been informed that in a very few states, arrowhead hunting in general on private land may be questionable and might require a permit from a state governmental agency. I have simply not had the time or resources available to me to research this topic in all fifty states of this country, and an entire book could be written on this topic alone. It is something, however, that a reader of this book should be aware of. Also, I have been told that in some states the law requires an arrowhead hunter to have written permission from the landowner on them at all times when hunting private land. It is sad to say that the time may almost have come where it will be necessary to consult a knowledgeable lawyer (maybe even a criminal lawyer) before one can safely go arrowhead hunting in certain states of this country. I must, therefore, advise all readers to thoroughly look into and research the legality of their activities.

In the western United States, when hunting artifacts on a private ranch with permission, one still has to be extremely cautious and aware of where you are hunting at all times. These ranches are quite often comprised of not only privately owned land (deeded land), but also leased government land from such agencies as the BLM or NFS. You can literally be hunting arrowheads legally on one side of a fence and not on the other, all within the same ranch you have permission to hunt on. In areas where there is no fence, you can imagine what a predicament you are in. The only answer is to obtain maps such as shown in illustrations 7 and 8. These maps will indicate privately owned land and government-owned land. You obviously have to be able to read these maps and know where you are at all times. One other alternative would be to ask the rancher where the private land stops and where the government land begins. Some inexperienced ranch hands might not know this information, so you have to be quite careful whom you are asking when you have no map available to you. You should also be aware that under ARPA, if you remove a stone artifact illegally in one state and travel home across a state line, you have committed another federal crime in doing so. One should, therefore, obtain a complete set of available maps for the area you will be hunting and become thoroughly familiar with them. Always remember, too, that questionable activity is just not worth

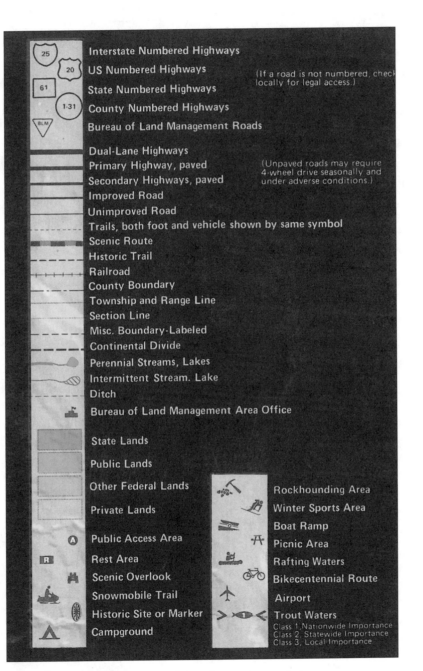

Interstate Numbered Highways

US Numbered Highways

(If a road is not numbered, check locally for legal access.)

State Numbered Highways

County Numbered Highways

Bureau of Land Management Roads

Dual-Lane Highways

Primary Highway, paved

(Unpaved roads may require 4-wheel drive seasonally and under adverse conditions.)

Secondary Highways, paved

Improved Road

Unimproved Road

Trails, both foot and vehicle shown by same symbol

Scenic Route

Historic Trail

Railroad

County Boundary

Township and Range Line

Section Line

Misc. Boundary-Labeled

Continental Divide

Perennial Streams, Lakes

Intermittent Stream. Lake

Ditch

Bureau of Land Management Area Office

State Lands

Public Lands

Other Federal Lands

Private Lands

Public Access Area

Rest Area

Scenic Overlook

Snowmobile Trail

Historic Site or Marker

Campground

Rockhounding Area

Winter Sports Area

Boat Ramp

Picnic Area

Rafting Waters

Bikecentennial Route

Airport

Trout Waters

Class 1, Nationwide Importance
Class 2, Statewide Importance
Class 3, Local Importance

Illustration 6   Bureau of Land Management map symbols.

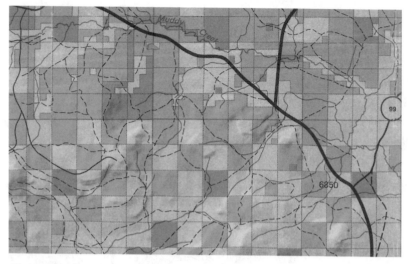

Illustration 7 Bureau of Land Management map.

Illustration 8 U.S. Geological Survey map.

taking the risk. Once you become the focus of an investigation, you run the risk of having your vehicle confiscated along with your entire collection of stone artifacts—not just the items in your vehicle, but your entire collection at home, too. The consequences from this point on are obvious, so it is not worth putting yourself in this situation. You simply have to be well educated, informed, and careful about your activities in the field. In many areas of the United States there is not nearly as much government land as there is in the West, so this predicament may not be as common in some areas of the country. But remember one thing—the federal law will be the same everywhere in the United States, and you may, in fact, have a problem if the land you have permission to hunt on is not all privately owned.

The same problem also exists with state-owned land, and, of course, state laws will vary from one state to another. If the area you have permission to hunt on is comprised of any land leased from a state, it will, no doubt, be unlawful to remove any stone artifacts from the state-owned land. This problem, likewise, could be present in any state of the United States. In the West, for example, under the rectangular survey system originally used to legally describe the land, each township is made up of thirty-six sections, and in each township, one section was designated originally as a State School Section that is owned by the state. I am not aware of how common this situation may be throughout the entire country, but in the West, it is certainly something to be aware of.

Historically, arrowhead hunters in the West have been known to kill rattlesnakes while out in the field—many artifact display frames contain the rattles taken from rattlesnakes—and I suspect that this activity occurs in other parts of the country, as well. I recently discovered that in Colorado it is now illegal to kill a rattlesnake out of season and without a license, and I would imagine that the same is true in other states, and perhaps also regarding other types of snakes. Again, a traditional activity sometimes associated with arrowhead hunting is now not only frowned upon, but illegal.

It is obvious from what I have set forth that people cannot be too careful with their artifact-hunting activities under existing law today. If in doubt about your planned activity, you should consult with the proper authorities, or in some cases, consult with an attorney. As unfortunate as this may be, it may be the only safe way to proceed.

CHAPTER 3

WHY LOOK FOR ARTIFACTS?

Most people who have found a beautiful arrowhead would agree that the excitement brought on by the discovery is the main reason they search for artifacts. Let's face it, finding any nice stone artifact can be a fun and very exciting experience, especially for those of us who respect history and how our ancestors lived years ago. For example, I have a tremendous respect for any stone age culture that survived because of the ability to create tools—mainly tools chipped from stone, which was the most obvious natural material they had to work with. It is true that many tools were made of wood, bone, and other "perishable" materials, but these materials gradually disintegrate on the surface of the ground and have long since disappeared, leaving only stone artifacts remaining to be found. Occasionally, bone or wood artifacts will show up in caves and other protected surface areas, but it is mainly the stone artifacts that withstand the elements and are not destroyed over time.

Stone artifacts, while generally resistant to weather and other natural forces, are quite often destroyed by animals. For instance, I have found many artifacts that have been stepped on and broken by cattle,

Illustration 9 The author's granddaughter Megan with her first arrowhead, found at age four.

Illustration 10   The author's weekend campsite on the Laramie plains in southern Wyoming.

deer, or perhaps other larger animals. Besides the excitement of finding even a broken artifact, this is another good reason why a person would look for artifacts—simply to find and preserve an artifact before it is broken or destroyed, and its archaeological value lost forever. One unique stone artifact found on the surface could very easily lead professional archaeologists to a valuable discovery under the surface after further investigation. A good many professional archaeologists will readily admit that the vast majority of valuable archaeological sites have been discovered by amateurs who afterwards notified professionals of their discovery. From what I have heard or read, I would estimate that clearly three-fourths of the primary archaeological sites were originally discovered and reported by amateurs. I have, likewise, found many stone artifacts in dirt roads, many of which had been run over by vehicles and broken. These artifacts were out of archaeological context, but, even though broken, were nonetheless exciting to find. It is amazing how many artifacts found on a dirt road are not yet broken, which are obviously even more exciting to find. Common sense leads to the obvious conclusion that these artifacts should be picked up and preserved before they are broken or destroyed by vehicular activity.

Illustration 11   The author's family on a weekend trip in northern Colorado.

However, most professional archaeologists are critical of those who remove stone artifacts from their archaeological context. This is the obvious reason one should not dig or excavate an archaeological site. Many artifacts, however, are no longer in their original archaeological context. Picking up such an artifact is, more than likely, not going to destroy valuable archaeological information. This is true not only of the arrowhead in the dirt road, but also of an artifact found in a riverbed. Studies and experiments have been conducted, and it has been shown that an artifact can move a remarkable distance in running water. It would be extremely difficult to determine from where such an artifact originally came. Such artifacts are oftentimes reburied in silt and sand, and there is really no valid reason I know of why such an artifact should not be picked up and preserved before it is lost forever.

Illustration 12   The author's granddaughters during a camping trip.

Preservation of artifacts that are totally out of archaeological context is just one more reason why one would search for them.

Hunting for stone artifacts can, and does, more than often than not, lead to a valuable educational experience. This is obviously true for the professional archaeologist, and it is also true for far more amateur archaeologists than most people would think. For example, I know many amateurs who are far more knowledgeable than I am. As mentioned before, this is the main reason I have revised and updated this book. My discoveries over the years have led me to more study and research, and, therefore, more knowledge of archaeology. True respect for prehistoric people and their survival, brought on by finding stone artifacts and learning more about them, is a valuable personal experience. A good many of today's professional archaeologists began as amateur arrowhead hunters who developed a profound interest in archaeology thereafter. Many have gone on to become quite prominent and have contributed greatly to our knowledge of archaeology and the study of prehistoric cultures.

Last, but certainly not least, arrowhead hunting has proven to be a very worthwhile, wholesome, and valuable family experience. In this day and age of lost and confused people, both young and old, this society needs more wholesome family activity. People, especially young people, need to cultivate and develop an interest in history and a respect for prehistoric cultures. Families need to be together, do things together, and learn something worthwhile while doing so. A camping experience with the family provides plenty of fresh air, exercise, and exposure to nature. There is nothing quite as refreshing as taking a walk with a child or grandchild early in the morning when camping and hunting for artifacts. A child's thirst for knowledge is readily apparent with question after question about the landscape and plant and animal life. Then, when a nice arrowhead is found, the questions really begin. An adult should appreciate the value of this experience and encourage this type of learning. This kind of activity is good for a family and might help keep a family together. Furthermore, it might give a young person a purpose in life and help divert him or her from unwholesome and destructive activity so prevalent in today's society. Finally, such activity might result in the development of a prominent scientist—even a professional archaeologist.

CHAPTER 4

THE "FLINT" MATERIALS

It has been said that there is hardly a stone material, or bone material for that matter, that someone somewhere and at some time did not use to make an artifact. As a general rule, prehistoric people used the best material available to make implements and tools. Perhaps some of the more obvious examples are as follows:

▲ Volcanic igneous material such as obsidian is widely found in the Pacific Northwest and other areas of the West. Stone artifacts of obsidian are common in Washington and Oregon and relatively scarce in Kansas and Missouri. In our collection, which includes probably thousands of pieces of flint material from northern Colorado and southern Wyoming, we have relatively few obsidian pieces. On the other hand, some collections in Nevada and Idaho consist, for the most part, of obsidian artifacts.

▲ Materials such as felsite and rhyolite are common in the eastern United States, and so, therefore, are artifacts made from these materials. However, in Colorado, felsite and rhyolite artifacts are relatively scarce.

▲ Petrified wood, which is more common in Colorado, Arizona, and New Mexico than in Iowa and Missouri, was used more commonly in artifacts in the former states than the latter. An artifact made of petrified wood is more common in Colorado than in Kansas.

▲ Some materials seem to be unique to one particular area. Silicified oil shale, for example, is native material in northwestern Colorado and southwestern Wyoming and was commonly used for projectile points and tools in these areas. I would suspect that this material would be quite scarce in many other parts of the United States.

▲ My research has indicated that a good portion of the Spanish Diggings material and Hartville Uplift material of east-central Wyoming was quartzite and chert, and, of course, the area is widely known as perhaps the largest quarry of its kind in the United States. Again, artifacts of this material seem to be more common in the inter-mountain states than in many other parts of the country. In the areas of northern Colorado and southern Wyoming that I have hunted, quartzite artifacts seem to be quite common, and a good share of this material was quarried in the Spanish Diggings. Some have suggested that many of the quartzite artifacts found throughout the inter-mountain region originally came from the famous Spanish Diggings or the Hartville Uplift areas of Wyoming. Chert or jasper from these areas is often brown or yellow with black specks throughout the stone.

When hunting artifacts, you generally look for what is loosely termed *flint*. I use the term *flint materials* rather loosely throughout this book for lack of a better overall term. What is carelessly identified as flint may actually be any one of the following materials: agate, chalcedony, jasper, chert, obsidian, petrified wood, quartz, quartzite, basalt,

Illustration 13   An assortment of various flint materials. Upper row from left to right: chalcedony, quartzite, chert; middle row from left to right: jasper, obsidian, basalt; lower row from left to right: agate, petrified wood, quartz.

or flint itself. An overall view of these materials together can be seen in illustration 13.

Agate has been described as chalcedony with an irregular and banded appearance. The bands may vary in coloration and be wavy or parallel. As with the flints, cherts, chalcedonies, and jaspers, agate will most often be translucent or opaque. A translucent stone will allow light to pass through it, while an opaque stone will not. You can actually see

Illustration 14   Agate.

through a transparent stone such as chalcedony. While I have few artifacts made from agate (see illustration 14), they may be easily found in
certain parts of the country. Many of the gem points from the Pacific
Northwest are actually agate and chalcedony points.

Chalcedony is sometimes transparent but normally is just translucent. It has been described as a waxy and smooth form of quartz vary-
ing in color from gray to white but can also be yellow, green, brown,
or blue. Most of the chalcedony artifacts that I have seen are clear to
white in color and are quite translucent—some even transparent. Other
forms of chalcedony may be reddish brown or red and, in my opinion,
would be quite difficult to distinguish from flint, jasper, or chert by anyone other than the experienced geologist. (See illustration 15.)

Jasper is an opaque blend of opal, chalcedony, and quartz that is
normally brown, green, red, yellow, or a mixture of these colors, with

Illustration 15   Chalcedony.

occasionally a banded appearance. Artifacts of jasper are relatively common, and, from my study, it would seem that many red and yellow artifacts are probably jasper. (See illustration 16.)

Chert is a sedimentary material and has been called an impure form of flint. It is usually gray, white, yellow, black, or brown and, except for the geologist, would be difficult for the average person to differentiate from flint, jasper, or chalcedony. Artifacts of chert are commonly found throughout the United States because it was one of the most widely used of all the flint materials. (See illustration 17.)

Illustration 16 Jasper.

Illustration 17 Chert.

Obsidian is an igneous material and has sometimes been called volcanic glass because it generally looks like glass, especially when broken. It is normally black, very shiny, and has sharp edges when broken that can easily cut a person. It is obvious why this material would be suitable for making projectile points and tools with its sharp, cutting edges. Because of its superior qualities, obsidian knives or scalpels have actually been used in modern-day surgeries and in some instances were found to be preferable over steel instruments. Larger pieces of obsidian are opaque, although thin flakes are translucent and many times even transparent. Another type of obsidian is brownish red in color and has been referred to as mahogany obsidian. A rougher, duller form of obsidian is called pitchstone, which was also used in making artifacts. Obsidian seems to be more common in the Pacific Northwest, although it can be found throughout the country, perhaps more frequently in mountainous regions where volcanoes may have existed. (See illustration 18.)

Basalt is another igneous volcanic material that has been used to make artifacts. It is similar to obsidian in color, although it is not nearly as shiny and smooth. It has been said that basalt is the most common stone found on Earth. I suppose it is easy to understand why it was used to make stone tools and arrowheads—it was probably always available to prehistoric peoples. (See illustration 13.)

Felsite is an igneous rock that has been described as a fine-grained quartz or feldspar. Felsite was commonly used for the manufacture of artifacts, perhaps where other flint materials were not readily available. I have seen a number of felsite artifacts from the Midwest but have not personally collected many from the Rocky Mountain area.

Petrified wood is an agatized or silicified wood and generally has flintlike shininess or glitter. Some specimens clearly reveal the grain of the original wood; most petrified wood is colorful and easy to identify. With its quartzlike nature, it was suitable for manufacture into artifacts. Crystals are often found in specimens of petrified wood, further indicating its quartzlike nature. Petrified wood can be almost any color, but most of the artifacts I have seen are generally red, brown, yellow, or a mixture of these colors. (See illustration 19.)

Illustration 18   Obsidian.

Although many of the materials discussed here could be loosely classified as being in the quartz or quartzite family, pure quartz artifacts are rare as opposed to artifacts made of flint, jasper, chert, or chalcedony. (See illustration 20.) Quartz artifacts that I have found are white and generally opaque and are delicately made. I have seen one collection of projectile points from Alabama that consisted entirely of quartz material. Apparently this material was the best material available in that area at the time of manufacture.

I have seen some artifacts made from a sedimentary material known as shale, but on the whole, this type of material was difficult to work and broke easily during manufacture. In our entire collection, we have only one arrowhead made of what appears to be shale. This arrowhead was found in a low-lying area near Cody, Wyoming, and as far as I am concerned, was a rare find, at least in this part of the country.

Quartzite was perhaps one of the most common of all the flint materials used for artifact manufacture and was probably more readily

Illustration 19   Petrified wood.

Illustration 20   Quartz.

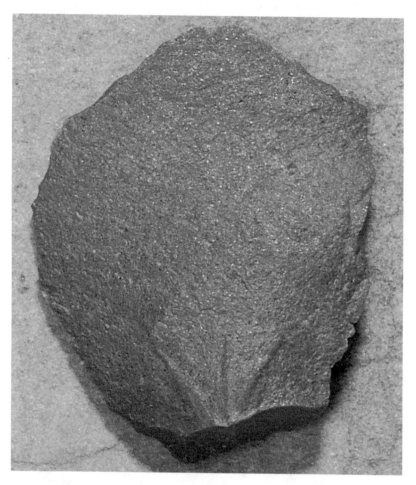

Illustration 21   Quartzite.

found throughout the country. Quartzite is a metamorphic material, is a member of the quartz family, and is usually gray to white, or brown, red, or yellow in color. It is generally more opaque than chalcedony and somewhat more grainy than jasper, chalcedony, or chert. Like the other flint materials, quartzite will generally stand out clearly in an open field, even among the presence of other rocks. On a sunny day in a dirt field, a piece of flint may be visible for 20 feet or more. (See illustration 21.)

WELL-KNOWN FLINT QUARRIES

The flint materials previously discussed are what I consider to be the primary materials used throughout the United States by early peoples. As might be expected, the first Americans had favorite stone quarries that they visited frequently because of the superior quality of material available. The Knife River flint quarries of southwestern North Dakota is a good example. Knife River flint is actually silicified lignite and has excellent qualities for flaking stone tools and projectile points. As further proof of the popularity of this material, artifacts of Knife River flint have been found all over the western part of the country and as far east as Ohio and Pennsylvania. The color of this material ranges from almost black to amber and brown. It is generally quite distinguishable from all other flint materials once you are familiar with it.

Another well-known material that is generally quite easy to recognize is alibates flint from the Alibates Flint Quarry located in the Texas panhandle north of Amarillo. This material is agatized dolomite and is most often white to gray in color, containing very colorful patterns of red, orange, yellow, and brown. It is not unusual to find stone artifacts made from this material throughout the plains of the Midwest, several hundred miles from the quarry. Today, this area has been set aside as the Alibates National Monument, and removing specimens from the quarry is against the law. Again, this material was highly sought after by prehistoric peoples because of the ease of flaking the material and perhaps, too, because of its colorful appearance.

As mentioned previously, the Spanish Diggings quarries, or the Hartville Uplift, as some refer to it, are located in east-central Wyoming. This area actually covers a significant amount of land, and a nice variety of flint materials are found therein. The primary materials, however, are quartzite and chert. As characteristic of the other well-known flint quarries, this material is scattered over a large area of the West, and it is not unusual to find artifacts made from this stone several hundred miles from the main quarry.

Prehistoric peoples literally mined flattop chert or chalcedony from a large natural outcropping of this material located in north-eastern Colorado and known as Flattop Butte. Most material of this type that I have seen is white to pink in color and is quite easy to recognize. It likewise has superior qualities that made it easy to work, and artifacts made from this material have also been found over a large area of the inter-mountain West.

Three other popular prehistoric stone quarries are located in the Edwards Plateau area of central Texas, Flint Hills of eastern Kansas, and Flint Ridge area of Ohio. I am not as familiar with these areas as I am with the areas previously mentioned. It is my understanding that fine quality material from these quarries was likewise highly sought after by the first Americans, and it is not unusual to find artifacts made from this material over a wide geographical area.

There are literally hundreds of natural outcroppings of flint materials located throughout the United States—some with popular names, and a great many that have never been named. For example, there are several small outcroppings of chert and quartzite located within a few miles of my home. Artifacts found here locally are oftentimes made from these local materials. These are what I refer to as "native" flint materials—materials found naturally in a given geographical area. This local material was often of poor quality and difficult to work by the prehistoric flintknapper. This is the primary reason why top-quality materials from the well-known quarries was highly sought after and transported great distances by early peoples. This material, after being transported, then becomes "foreign" flint material in a given area and is almost always an indication of prehistoric activity.

Flint materials were most suitable for artifact manufacture because of their characteristic conchoidal fracture upon the application of pressure. *Conchoidal fracture* means that the material breaks in a circular or semicircular manner rather than along a straight line or cleavage plane. Most of the materials discussed in this chapter will fracture conchoidally. The conchoidal fracture is basically a cuplike depression with concentric semicircular lines throughout the depressed area. The trained eye can spot this type of breakage in a rock from a distance of several feet. (See illustration 22.)

The following is a general listing (not meant to be all-inclusive) of several of the more well-known localized flint materials found throughout the United States:

Illustration 22   Three pieces of flint material that show variations of the typical conchoidal fracture resulting in the cuplike depressions.

- ▲ Obsidian—Glass Butte, Oregon
- ▲ Obsidian, pitchstone, basalt—Coconino County, Arizona
- ▲ Agatized coral and chert—Florida
- ▲ Crescent chert—Missouri
- ▲ Burlington chert—Illinois
- ▲ Georgetown flint and chert—Georgetown, Texas
- ▲ Plate chalcedony—southwestern South Dakota
- ▲ Porcellainite (siltstone)—north-central Wyoming and south-central Montana
- ▲ Hixton quartzite—Oshkosh, Wisconsin
- ▲ Silicified slate—Stanly County, North Carolina
- ▲ Coarse quartzite—Virginia
- ▲ Indiana hornestone—Kentucky

▲ Novaculites—Arkansas

▲ Andesite—New Jersey

▲ Flint Hill quartzite—southwestern South Dakota

▲ Jurassic Morrison formation chert and quartzite—
Bighorn Mountains, Wyoming

▲ Silicified oil shale—northwestern Colorado, southwestern Wyoming

▲ Silicified oolite—Red Desert, Wyoming

▲ Niobrara jasper—southwestern Nebraska, northwestern Kansas

▲ Tecovas jasper—Texas panhandle

▲ Nehawka-Pennsylvania chert—eastern Nebraska

CHAPTER 5

HOW ARTIFACTS WERE MADE

In looking for flint materials and stone artifacts, it helps considerably if you have some basic knowledge of how the artifact was made by the prehistoric flintknapper. This helps, of course, in recognizing an artifact as well as the by-product chips and flakes from the making of the artifact. Illustration 23 gives an indication of how to recognize the man-made flakes of flint in their natural state. A piece of raw material appearing naturally may seem to be just another rock with a smooth outside surface somewhat irregular in shape. Once the stone has been worked, however, as shown in illustration 24, and a chip has flaked off, the resulting flake, as shown in illustration 23, is readily identified as being man-made. The inner face, designated by the letter *a* in the illustration, is usually concave, somewhat smooth, and often contains semicircular lines evidencing the characteristic conchoidal fracture. Once struck, these flakes provided the basic piece for the arrowhead, knife, or other tool, depending upon the size, thickness, and degree of concavity or curvature.

Generally, three primary methods of working stone were used by the prehistoric flintknapper: direct percussion, indirect percussion, and pressure flaking.

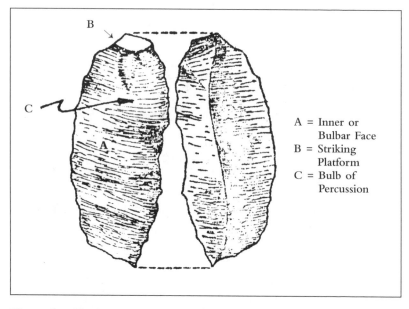

A = Inner or
    Bulbar Face
B = Striking
    Platform
C = Bulb of
    Percussion

Illustration 23   Man-made flake of flint. Courtesy Stackpole Company, Harrisburg, Pennsylvania.

Illustration 24   A flint core showing what is left after removal of many flakes or spalls.

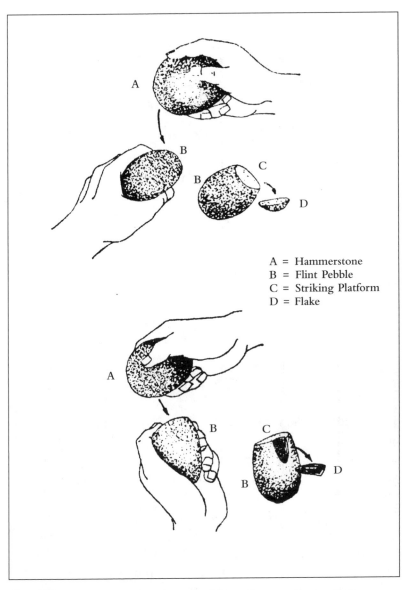

A = Hammerstone
B = Flint Pebble
C = Striking Platform
D = Flake

Illustration 25   Striking platform for flaking. Courtesy Stackpole Company, Harrisburg, Pennsylvania.

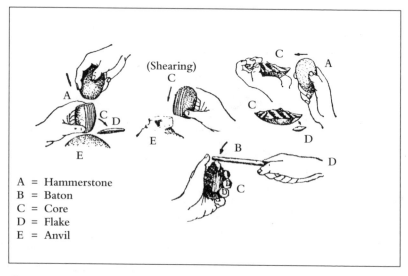

Illustration 26   Methods of direct percussion. Courtesy Stackpole Company, Harrisburg, Pennsylvania.

DIRECT PERCUSSION

The first method, direct percussion, was used primarily, although not exclusively, to rough out or break down larger flint material into workable smaller pieces. The large piece of flint material was broken down from the size of a volleyball into several smaller pieces. This was usually accomplished by directly striking the larger piece with one end of a hammerstone, thereby causing an unnatural or man-made fracture of the core material, sometimes called the "mother stone" or "mother flint." On occasion, the core itself was held in the hand and hit against a large stone known as a stone anvil, thereby breaking off smaller, more workable pieces known as flakes or spalls. Once in a while, direct percussion was used in finish or retouching work, but this was the exception rather than the rule. The methods of direct percussion are shown in illustration 26.

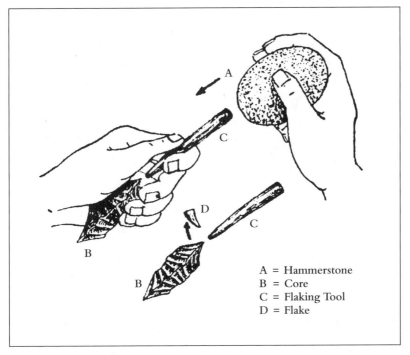

A = Hammerstone
B = Core
C = Flaking Tool
D = Flake

Illustration 27   Methods of indirect percussion. Courtesy Stackpole Company, Harrisburg, Pennsylvania.

INDIRECT PERCUSSION

Indirect percussion was ordinarily, though not always, used to rough out or shape an artifact to the point where it was readily recognizable as an artifact. Indirect percussion involved striking an intermediate handheld tool against the core or flake to shape an artifact. The hammerstone was generally used as the striking tool, and antler, bone, or wood was used as the intermediate, handheld flaking tool. The antler, for example, was hit on the flat end with the hammerstone, thereby forcing the more pointed end into the handheld core or flake, in turn causing smaller chips or flakes to break off conchoidally from the future artifact. (See illustration 27.)

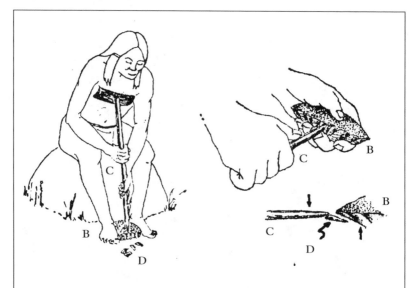

Left: Worker punches blades (D) off the core (B) by leaning his body on long stick with breast rest (C).
Right: Worker presses pointed tool (C) against surface of stone (B) and twists. Flake (D) is detached from underside of stone

Illustration 28   Methods of pressure flaking. Courtesy Stackpole Company, Harrisburg, Pennsylvania.

PRESSURE FLAKING

Pressure flaking was the delicate technique used to retouch or put the final touch or edge on an artifact. Most beautifully worked artifacts were pressure flaked around the edges during construction. In pressure flaking, the antler, bone, or wood tool was pressed firmly against the stone, usually along the edges, and at the same time twisted or rotated to one side or another. The tiny flake or chip detached from the underside or face opposite from where the pressure was applied. Perhaps the finest example of pressure flaking is the finely "honed" edge of the classical Folsom point shown in illustration 4. Illustration 28 shows the methods of pressure flaking that resulted in the finely worked thumb scraper and knife shown in illustration 29.

In recognizing worked flint material, you must remember two basic concepts in stone-artifact construction: bifacial and unifacial working. *Bifacial working* means that an artifact has been worked or chipped on both sides, while *unifacial working* indicates that only one side has been worked. Many small- or medium-size thumb scrapers, such as those shown in illustrations 65 and 66, are unifacial in construction. Some stone knives and relatively few arrowheads are unifacial in character; the majority are bifacial. Some scrapers, usually the larger ones, are bifacially worked and are thicker and rougher in appearance than most knives or arrowheads. Usually, but not always, the unworked side of the unifacial artifact is somewhat concave, such as is shown in illustration 23.

A preform is a rather small- or medium-size, thin, leaf-shaped piece of flint material that can easily be mistaken for a small knife, scraper, or triangular notchless arrowhead. The flintknapper broke down larger pieces of flint into blades or flakes for easier transportation. These blades or flakes were then worked generally into a leaf-shaped piece that could be easily worked into an arrowhead at some future time. In illustration 30, the preform is shown in the various ways in which it could be refined and notched into a specific arrowhead.

Illustration 29   Small thumb scraper (left) and small knife (right), showing the delicate and finely touched workmanship resulting from the pressure-flaking technique.

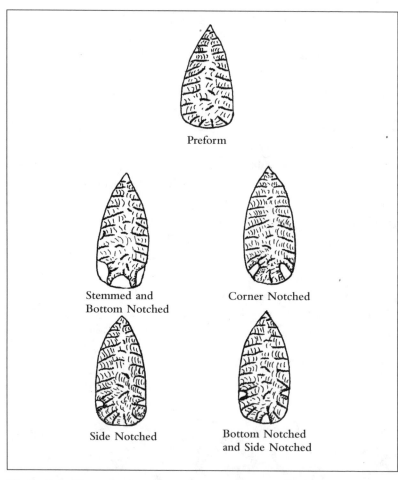

Preform

Stemmed and
Bottom Notched

Corner Notched

Side Notched

Bottom Notched
and Side Notched

Illustration 30 Examples of the various notch types and styles for arrowheads that could result from the same preform.

Flintknapping, or lithic technology, is surprisingly complex. A thorough reading of books on flintknapping (see bibliography) reveals the technical aspects and application of many of the principles of physics. A thorough study of how artifacts were made goes well beyond the scope of this book. See also chapter 10, on modern-day flintknapping.

CHAPTER 6

ARROWHEAD, SPEARPOINT, OR KNIFE?

A thorough study of archaeology reveals a remarkable similarity between arrowheads, spearpoints, and knives. When you really stop to think about it, just about any arrowhead or spearpoint could have also been used as a knife, especially if it were hafted onto a wood, horn, or bone handle. Hafting is often aided by the presence of notches in the stone projectile point or tool, although this is not always true. Many stone knives without notches were hafted to a handle. Similarly, many stone knives, with or without notches, could have simply been held in the hand and used effectively. The discovery of hafted stone knives in dry caves has proven that many large, notched points previously thought to be spearpoints or large arrowheads were actually used as knives. When one of these larger stone points is found unhafted on the surface of the ground, you may simply have to speculate as to how it was used. There is also the possibility that it may have been used as both a knife and projectile point, perhaps even by different cultures at different times over a great number of years. Illustration 35 depicts a point that probably could have been used as either a spearpoint or hafted knife. It is, no doubt, too big to be classified as an arrowhead.

The point in illustration 36 is easily too large to be used as an arrow-head. In the first edition of this book I referred to this point as a spear-point; I have learned, however, that this point was more likely used as a hafted knife. It may well be too wide to have ever been used as any type of projectile point.

THE ARROWHEAD

The arrowhead is found in a great variety of sizes, shapes, materials, and colors, depending upon several factors: (1) the type of prehistoric culture that made the arrowhead, (2) the area of the country involved, (3) the available material, and (4) the proposed use of the arrowhead. It has been speculated that certain cultures made arrowheads only in certain ways, and from my study, this is generally true. It must be remembered, however, that identical arrowheads found in completely different parts of the United States could have been made by totally separate and unique cultures that existed hundreds of miles and numerous years apart. Certain types of arrowheads are, however, more commonly found in some parts of the country than in others, depending upon the availability of stone. The obsidian arrowhead and gem point made of agate, jasper, and the more colorful stones are far more common in Oregon and the Pacific Northwest, where these materials are more abundant. In northern Colorado, by contrast, obsidian deposits are difficult to find. By the same token, an arrowhead made of white quartz can more likely be found in the northern Colorado mountains than in some other states, where quartz is not as common. Likewise, an arrowhead made of petrified wood would probably be more common in Arizona, New Mexico, or Colorado than in a Great Plains state. An arrowhead made from quartzite might be found in almost every state, since quartzite is one of the most commonly available materials throughout the country. The same is true with all the various cherts, which are widely available.

ARROWHEAD TERMINOLOGY

In the study and collecting of arrowheads, you should first become familiar with general arrowhead terminology, as shown in illustration 31. The various parts of an arrowhead consist primarily of the tip or point, the center section or body, and the bottom or base, including the notches. The bevel is the slope or slant of the surface or face of the edge of the arrowhead at each side.

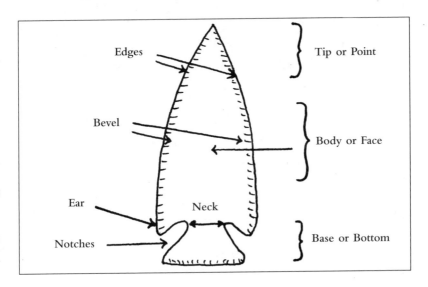

Illustration 31   Basic arrowhead terminology.

ARROWHEAD NOTCH TYPES

Arrowheads are generally classified according to the following notch types: (1) side notched, (2) bottom notched, (3) corner notched, (4) corner notched and bottom notched, (5) side notched and bottom notched, (6) stemmed and bottom notched, and (7) notchless, either triangular or oblong in shape—sometimes called "stemmed" or "shouldered." (See illustration 34.)

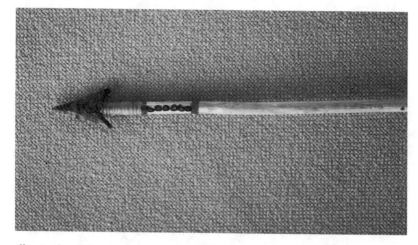

Illustration 32   Contemporary hafted arrowhead on shaft made by George Stewart of Windsor, Colorado.

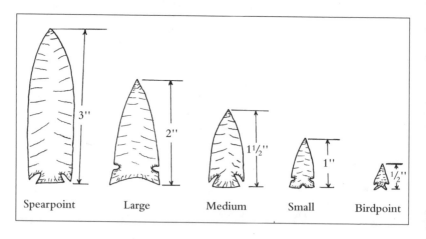

Illustration 33   General spearpoint and arrowhead sizes.

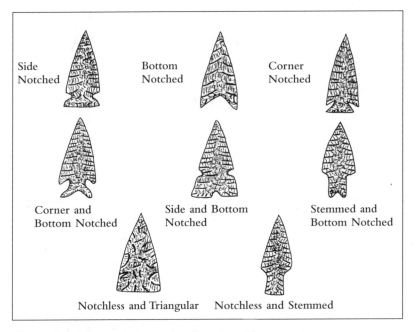

Side Notched

Bottom Notched

Corner Notched

Corner and Bottom Notched

Side and Bottom Notched

Stemmed and Bottom Notched

Notchless and Triangular   Notchless and Stemmed

Illustration 34   Typical arrowhead notch and base types.

Again, certain notch types are more common to some areas than others, and yet on one ridge in the northern Colorado foothills, all six notch types were found on the surface in a rather limited area. This suggests an area that was either heavily inhabited or hunted by a variety of prehistoric people over a period of years, or an area in which a particular culture lived and made many different types of arrowheads.

Archaeologists, both professional and amateur, have categorized arrowheads over the years based primarily on notch types. It is the notching of an arrowhead, along the sides or at the base, that gives it its individuality and makes it distinguishable from another. Hence, it is much more informative and interesting to find the base of arrowhead, rather than the tip. Obviously, most tips are the same, except for general size and flaking pattern, and you cannot normally determine from the tip what kind of base the arrowhead originally had. It should also be noted that in certain instances, the flaking pattern is also quite important in categorizing a particular projectile point. This is especially true when the overall shape is similar.

THE SPEARPOINT

The spearpoint is sometimes referred to as a large arrowhead, although more often than not, the spearpoint lacks notches for use in hafting. Effective hafting without notches was accomplished by grinding or smoothing the sharp edges at the basal end of the point and the base itself. This grinding of edges was accomplished by the use of a stone abrader (see chapter 7). The ground edges helped prevent the cutting of the hafting material (such as sinew) during the hafting process. With experience, one can actually feel the difference between the original flaked edge and the ground edge of the point. Also, some spearpoints, such as the classic Folsom point, were sometimes not very large in size. Not all Paleo points were several inches long, and many were quite narrow, such as the Eden point. Most Paleo spearpoints were stemmed or shouldered with ground edges and were hafted generally not at the end of the spear shaft itself but at the end of a foreshaft, such as is shown in illustration 39. The foreshaft was then inserted in the end of the spearshaft, as shown in illustration 38. More often than not, the entire spear was then thrown by the user with the aid of an atlatl, such as shown in illustration 40. The atlatl handle was probably wrapped with rawhide to aid in gripping, and the atlatl was often used with a stone weight, which added balance and weight to aid in the actual thrusting motion. The back end of the spearshaft was indented to allow insertion of the hook or spur of the atlatl. The entire assemblage of component parts was then held and balanced prior to the throw of the spear itself. Professional archaeological investigations have clearly shown that foreshafts were commonly used. A prehistoric hunter of large mammoths and bison would have had a real problem carrying a large number of spears while hunting on foot. A person carrying one or two spears and a bundle of foreshafts with hafted points would be better equipped for

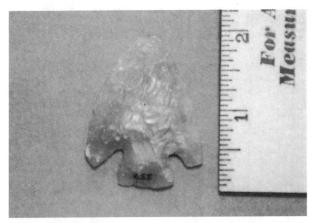

Illustration 35 Spearpoint or arrowhead? Large point found by author in 1980.

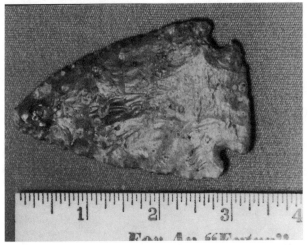

Illustration 36 Spearpoint or knife? Large point found by Mrs. Judy Wood of Cedaredge, Colorado, in 1982.

hunting. Such foreshafts were also used with arrows in the same manner after the bow and arrow came into common use. Spearshafts or arrows could be retrieved and used again with new foreshafts and points, assuming the used foreshaft was lost or the point broken. When you stop to think about this, it makes sense. Archaic spearpoints generally looked more like a large arrowhead, and many contained notches for

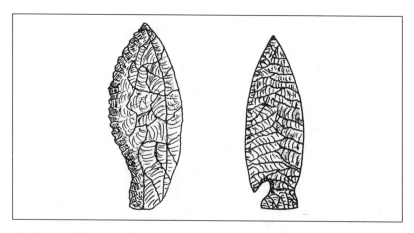

Illustration 37 Two hafted knives commonly mistaken for arrowheads or spearpoints. The knife at right has sometimes been referred to as a *slitter*.

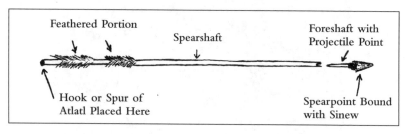

Illustration 38 Spearshaft.

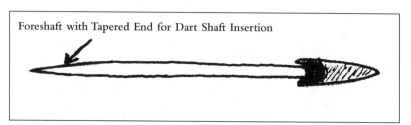

Illustration 39 Foreshaft.

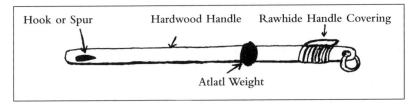

Hook or Spur   Hardwood Handle   Rawhide Handle Covering

Atlatl Weight

Illustration 40   Atlatl.

hafting. Some again, no doubt, may have been used as hafted knives. Generally speaking, though, many were used as spearpoints before the invention of the bow and arrow and the common use of arrowheads in more recent times. One more interesting thing to note is that a spearpoint hafted to a foreshaft could have easily been retrieved once an animal was down and then used as a hafted knife in the skinning and butchering processes. This again shows how arrowheads, spearpoints, and knives were interrelated and used often in more than one manner. When a person today finds a nice arrowhead or spearpoint, he or she may have also found a nice stone knife.

BROKEN ARROWHEADS AND SPEARPOINTS

When hunting arrowheads, a person will generally find eight to ten broken arrowheads for each perfect arrowhead found. You should, therefore, constantly be looking for flint materials with the characteristic shapes of the tip, the center section, or the base. It is very easy to walk right over or even step on a part of an arrowhead and not even know it. To the untrained eye, the center section of an arrowhead may appear as just another small piece of flint not worth bending over to pick up. The tip and base, of course, are more easily recognized as once being part of a larger arrowhead. Various parts of arrowheads are depicted in illustration 41 in such a manner to also indicate what the entire arrowhead once looked like before it was broken. You should actually memorize the various base styles, for this is the key to spotting arrowheads or parts of them in the field.

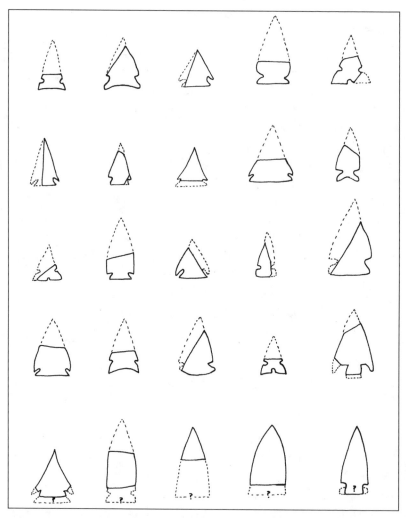

Illustration 41   Commonly found arrowhead pieces.

REWORKED PROJECTILE POINTS

With the large number of broken projectile points still being found today, it is logical to assume that even a few thousand years ago there were many broken points and tools already on the ground. One culture of prehistoric people no doubt found stone artifacts left behind by previous cultures. Oftentimes these artifacts were also found broken; then reworked and used again—sometimes for a totally different purpose than originally intended. Prehistoric people also retrieved their own broken projectile points and damaged stone tools. When desirable stone material was not readily available, broken points and tools were easily and quickly reworked by a skilled flintknapper and used again. Today, I find that a good many of the stone tools I have found together with many projectile points have been reworked at one time or another, sometimes more than once. Also, many small stone knives have been sharpened over and over again and are now perhaps only one-fourth as large as they were originally. An original good-size arrowhead could today be discovered as a smaller arrowhead, a drill, or a hafted scraper, and an artifact that began as a spearpoint could now be a notched arrowhead. Folsom points have been found with notches flintknapped by a later prehistoric culture. I have personally found reworked Allen points and Scottsbluff points only 1 inch long. They were initially, no doubt, several inches long. I have often joked that I will never find a "whole" Paleo point 3 or 4 inches long!

Illustration 42 has been included to show how six large projectile points could be found today as smaller points or entirely different tools—graver, hafted scraper (or knife), and drill. Illustration 43 shows five recently discovered reworked projectile points that are much smaller than originally made. In order to determine if an artifact has been reworked, look for a disparity in width versus length, or perhaps a crookedness of appearance—not all of these artifacts were reworked excellently. In other words, if you find a "whole" arrowhead that is wider than it is long, an Allen point only an inch long, or an arrowhead that is lopsided or not symmetrical, it has more than likely been

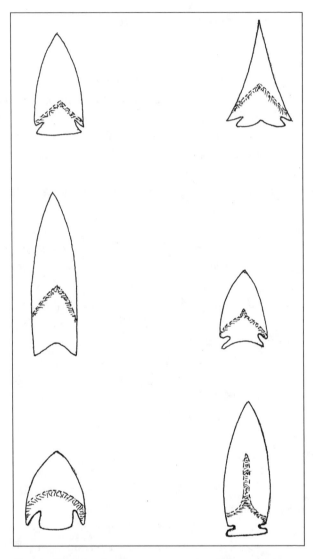

Illustration 42   Reworked projectile points. The point at center right has been reworked into a graver; at the lower left, the point has been reworked into a hafted scraper; and the point at the lower right has been reworked into a hafted drill.

Illustration 43   Reworked projectile points in author's family collection. The large point in the center is probably a broken knife that has been reworked or sharpened more than once. The point at the upper right is a Paleo point that was probably reworked at a much later date because of the "freshness" in flaking in the area of the tip. Although hard to see, the point at the lower left was reworked into a graver that may have been hafted.

reworked. Of course, sometimes it can be almost impossible to determine if something has been reworked, especially if the workmanship is of very high quality. Sometimes, especially if one uses a magnifying glass, it is quite easy to see a difference in the flaking pattern on the artifact. The reworked portion will often have a more fresh appearance or even a sharper feel to it than that of the original flaking. The reworked area may also contain what are known as "step fractures" in the stone. Only through learning and experience can one truly distinguish reworked stone artifacts, and eventually the day will come when you will be able to determine this immediately. It's nice to know the difference.

Hafted Scraper

Broken Arrowhead

Illustration 44   The broken arrowhead on the right was reworked into the hafted scraper on the left, resulting in what has been referred to by some as a "stunner."

THE "STUNNER," "POISON POINT," AND "BIRDPOINT"

The arrowhead commonly known as the "stunner," or "bunt," is perhaps one of the more puzzling artifacts (illustration 44). You must be careful in classifying an arrowhead as a stunner, because frequently the tip of an arrowhead may be broken in such a manner, giving it the appearance of a stunner. This false appearance usually results from a shattering fracture of the tip rather than a good, clean break. The so-called stunner, on close examination, will reveal careful, deliberate, and delicate workmanship into a rounded tip rather than a point.

The so-called stunner gets its name from speculation that it was shot with a bow and arrow to merely stun or daze an animal, rather than to penetrate or kill. Personally, I think that the stunner was hafted onto a short shaft and used as a knife, gouge, or scraper for removing marrow from bones or other similar tasks, because I have yet to hear or read of a reason why anyone would ever want to just stun an animal. In addition, some small scrapers have been found that were actually notched for attachment to a shaft. These can usually be distinguished from the so-called stunner because they are generally worked only on one side and look like a scraper rather than an arrowhead or knife. Hafted scrapers are described in more detail in chapter 7.

Illustration 45 The common notchless arrowhead or knife (center), which some call a "poison point."

A so-called poison point can allegedly be almost any arrowhead that was used to poison an animal as well as pierce its hide. Most so-called poison points were notchless and triangular in shape so the arrowhead could detach easily and remain in the wound in case the shaft of the arrow should be jarred loose or fall. In order to poison the animal, supposedly the arrowhead would have been previously soaked in rattlesnake venom or baked in decayed meat. Another speculated method of poisoning was to imbed an arrowhead in a detached animal liver, place the liver on an anthill, and let the liver decay while at the same time being constantly bitten by the ants. Some steel arrowheads were left to rust before being baked in decayed meat.

I personally feel that most triangular, notchless arrowheads were actually hafted onto a shaft in a firm manner without the help of notches and were simply used in the same manner as any other arrowhead—not really as the so-called poison point. In most cases, if an animal is struck in the right places by a projectile point, there would be no reason for a person to go to all of this trouble and preparation to poison an animal. The "poison point" is shown in illustration 45.

The so-called birdpoint firstly gets its name from its small size, and secondly from the notion that it was only used for hunting birds and other small game animals. While this may be generally true, one must keep in mind that a birdpoint could have easily been used to hunt buffalo or other large game animals, as well. If an animal is struck in the right place, even a birdpoint can kill it, even if it is a large animal such as a buffalo. This is probably even more true if several birdpoints penetrate the animal. I am personally familiar with one buffalo kill site in northern Colorado where the vast majority of the points found were birdpoints. This is just one example of when modern archaeological studies have disproven age-old concepts, such as categorizing all small arrowheads as "birdpoints." Nevertheless, birdpoint is a commonly used term in the field and is probably as good a way as any to quickly describe what has been discovered.

THE SERRATED ARROWHEAD

Another type of arrowhead that, in my opinion, is rarely found in the areas with which I am familiar is the serrated edge point, shown in illustration 46. Although I have seen many pictures of these arrowheads, I can recall very few such points being found in perfect condition in northern Colorado or southern Wyoming in recent years. I have found a few broken serrated points, but a whole serrated point is difficult to find. Generally, the edge of an arrowhead is one continuous plane from base to tip, with no indentations unless chipped or broken. The serrated-edge arrowhead will have many small, uniform indentations along each edge in a sawtoothlike pattern. It would seem that such a point would have been very difficult to make and would have required meticulous workmanship. Some authorities believe this artifact was used as a knife rather than an arrowhead. In such cases, it was probably used by being hafted onto a shaft rather than simply held in the hand. Other authorities believe that such an artifact may have been ceremonial in nature.

THE METAL ARROWHEAD

As caucasians began to settle this country, especially when trappers and fur traders began to penetrate the Midwest and West, the steel arrowhead came into common usage. The effectiveness and durability of such an arrowhead is readily apparent; even today, steel-tipped arrows are widely used in bow hunting. The era of the steel-tipped arrow was

Illustration 46   A serrated arrowhead showing finely worked serrations on each edge of the point, resulting in a saw-toothed appearance at the edges.

short-lived, however, because of the almost simultaneous introduction of firearms. The steel arrowhead is a rare find because of the more rapid oxidation, or rusting, of steel over the years, as compared to little, if any, deterioration of the stone or flint-type materials of the classic arrowhead. (See illustration 47 for two types of steel arrowhead found by a homesteader years ago in southern Wyoming.)

PROJECTILE POINT IDENTIFICATION GUIDE

Illustration 49 will give you a general idea of some of the various types of arrowheads and spearpoints found throughout the United States. Many of those shown are quite similar and are hard to differentiate from other projectile points. Often, the same arrowhead may be named differently depending on the part of the country in which it is found and the culture from which it came. For instance, I have focused

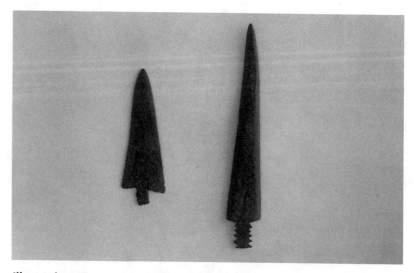

Illustration 47   Two examples of the typical steel arrowhead used on the western plains in the late 1800s.

my illustrations on projectile points with which I am more familiar. Cultures such as the Hohokam, Hopewell, Adena, Fremont, Desert, Basket Maker, Pueblo, various eastern U.S. cultures, and a number of cultures in Texas and the southern United States are evidenced by a number of other locally named projectile points. Many of these are very similar to those illustrated herein but have different names.

Generally, the projectile points illustrated are categorized according to the general age of the artifact into Paleo points, Archaic points, and Woodland points. The older projectile points are Paleo points and are spearpoints rather than arrowheads, having been made and used before the bow and arrow. Much of the finer workmanship is found in Paleo points. Most of the commonly used names of Paleo points are generally accepted throughout the United States.

Archaic points are not as old as Paleo points but are older than Woodland points. Many arrowheads found today as surface finds are hard to classify as either Archaic or Woodland, unless, of course, you have found an arrowhead that has an obvious point name that is associated with a well-known culture.

Illustration 48 Various assorted arrowheads and artifacts found on one ranch in southern Wyoming. Note the different types of flint materials and notch types of arrowheads found in the same general location. Also note the scrapers made for hafting onto a shaft in the upper left and upper right corners. The top row also contains a typical bifacial knife, second from the left, and a unifacial crescent, second from the right, with a somewhat crude drill between the knives.

The projectile points illustrated are not inclusive of every point ever found. However, they do include many of the commonly found points in the United States and, more particularly, in the western part of the country. On the other hand, many of the points shown are extremely rare and hard to find, especially those shown as Paleo points.

In many cases, the flaking technique used on the face of the point or along the edges and base of the point is the primary characteristic used to categorize or classify the artifact. Illustration 49 does not purport to show all the intricacies of flaking techniques, but merely the various general shapes or styles of projectile points. In many cases, professional assistance may be needed to classify a point, and even then, all authorities may not be in agreement.

For a more detailed and excellent description of all the projectile points typically found throughout the United States, read the identification guides listed in the bibliography at the end of this book.

Chronological Sequence of Archaeological Time Periods

Pre–Clovis	pre–10,000 B.C.
Early Paleo	10,000 B.C. to 7,500 B.C.
Paleo	7,500 B.C. to 6,500 B.C.
Late Paleo	6,500 B.C. to 5,000 B.C.
Early Archaic	6,000 B.C. to 3,000 B.C.
Middle Archaic	4,000 B.C. to 2,000 B.C.
Late Archaic–Early Woodland	2,000 B.C. to 1,000 B.C.
Woodland–Late Prehistoric	1,000 B.C. to A.D. 1,500
Historic	A.D. 1,500 to present

Because archaeology is not an exact science, there are various opinions concerning the time periods, and the overlapping of the time periods, shown. With no written record available, conjecture concerning these time periods cannot be avoided.

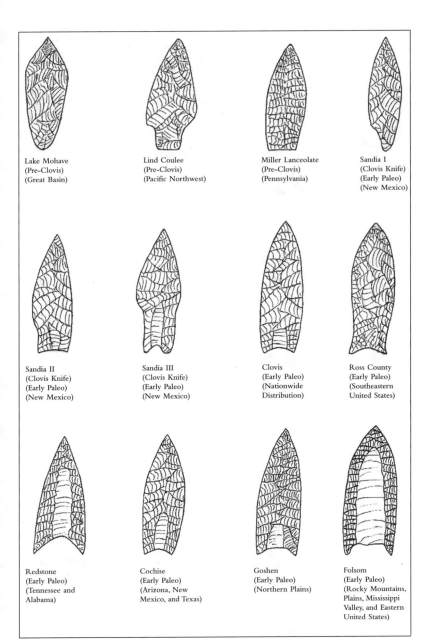

Lake Mohave
(Pre-Clovis)
(Great Basin)

Lind Coulee
(Pre-Clovis)
(Pacific Northwest)

Miller Lanceolate
(Pre-Clovis)
(Pennsylvania)

Sandia I
(Clovis Knife)
(Early Paleo)
(New Mexico)

Sandia II
(Clovis Knife)
(Early Paleo)
(New Mexico)

Sandia III
(Clovis Knife)
(Early Paleo)
(New Mexico)

Clovis
(Early Paleo)
(Nationwide
Distribution)

Ross County
(Early Paleo)
(Southeastern
United States)

Redstone
(Early Paleo)
(Tennessee and
Alabama)

Cochise
(Early Paleo)
(Arizona, New
Mexico, and Texas)

Goshen
(Early Paleo)
(Northern Plains)

Folsom
(Early Paleo)
(Rocky Mountains,
Plains, Mississippi
Valley, and Eastern
United States)

Illustration 49a   Projectile point identification guide.

Midland
(Early Paleo)
(Great Plains)

Beaver Lake
(Early Paleo)
(Tennessee, Kentucky,
Mississippi, and
Alabama)

Holcombe
(Early Paleo)
(Indians, Ohio,
and Michigan)

Debert
(Early Paleo)
(Maine and
Nova Scotia)

Plainview
(Paleo)
(Great Plains and
Rocky Mountains)

Dalton Colbert
(Paleo)
(Tennessee and
Alabama)

Dalton Greenbrier
(Paleo)
(Missouri and Illinois)

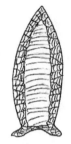

Cumberland
(Paleo)
(Mississippi, Tennessee,
Kentucky, and
Alabama)

Browns Valley
(Paleo)
(Mississippi Valley)

Hi-Lo
(Paleo)
(Indiana, Ohio, and
Michigan)

Hardaway
(Paleo)
(North Carolina)

Gypsum Cave
(Paleo)
(Nevada, Utah,
Arizona, and
Colorado)

Illustration 49b

Quad
(Paleo)
(Tennessee, Alabama,
and Kentucky)

Pelican
(Paleo)
(Northeast Texas,
Louisiana, Arkansas,
and Southeast
Oklahoma)

Wheeler Triangular
(Paleo)
(Tennessee, Georgia,
North and South
Carolina, and Alabama)

Wheeler Recurvate
(Paleo)
(Tennessee, Alabama,
and Georgia)

Breckenridge
(Paleo)
(Oklahoma,
Arkansas,
and Missouri)

Milnesand
(Paleo)
(New Mexico, West
Texas, Oklahoma,
and Plains States)

Meserve
(Paleo)
(Great Plains)

Agate Basin
(Paleo)
(Great Plains
and Midwest)

Hell Gap
(Paleo)
(Rocky Mountains
and Northern Plains)

Alberta
(Paleo)
(Northern Great Plains)

Alberta/Cody I
(Paleo)
(Northern Great Plains)

Alberta/Cody II
(Paleo)
(Northern Great Plains)

Illustration 49c

Scottsbluff
(Paleo)
(Rocky Mountains
and Great Plains)

Eden
(Paleo)
(Rocky Mountains
and Great Plains)

Greenbrier
(Paleo)
(Kentucky, Tennessee,
and Alabama)

Firstview
(Paleo)
(Great Plains)

San Jon
(Paleo)
(Great Plains)

Kersey
(Paleo)
(Great Plains)

Frederick
(Late Paleo)
(Great Plains and
Rocky Mountains)

Allen
(Late Paleo)
(Rocky Mountains)

Angostura
(Late Paleo)
(Rocky Mountains
and Great Plains)

Lusk
(Late Paleo)
(Northern Plains)

Golondrina
(Late Paleo)
(Centeral and Southern
Texas)

Nebo Hill
(Late Paleo)
(Missouri and
Oklahoma)

Illustration 49d

Sedalia
(Late Paleo)
(Oklahoma, Mis-
souri,
and Illinois)

Rio Grande
(Jay)
(Late Paleo)
(Colorado and
New Mexico)

Silver Lake
(Early Archaic)
(Southwestern
United States)

Abilene
(Early Archaic)
(Texas and
Southwestern
United States)

Pinto Basin
(Early Archaic)
(Colorado, Utah,
Rocky Mountains,
and Southwestern
United States)

Hawken Side Notch
(Logan Creek)
(Early Archaic)
(Nebraska, Wyoming,
Pacific Northwest,
and Great Plains)

Oxbow
(Middle Archaic)
(Colorado and
Rocky Mountains)

McKean
(Middle Archaic)
(Rocky Mountains
and Northern Plains)

Calf Creek
(Middle Archaic)
(Oklahoma, Kansas,
Arkansas, Missouri,
and Great Plains)

Pryor
(Middle Archaic)
(Rocky Mountains
and Northern Plains)

Duncan
(Middle Archaic)
(Rocky Mountains
and Northern Plains)

Hanna
(Middle Archaic)
(Rocky Mountains
and Northern Plains)

Illustration 49e

Mallory
(Middle Archaic)
(Rocky Mountains
and Northern Plains)

Yonkee
(Middle Archaic)
(Rocky Mountains
and Northern Plains)

Green River
(Middle Archaic)
(Rocky Mountains
and Northern Plains)

Pelican Lake
(Glendo)
(Middle Archaic)
(Rocky Mountains
and Northern Plains)

Besant
(Late Archaic)
(Rocky Mountains
and Northern Plains)

Avonlea
(Late Archaic)
(Rocky Mountains
and Northern Plains)

Hogback
(Glendo)
(Woodland)
(Rocky Mountains
and Northern Plains)

Waubesa
(Woodland)
(Great Plains)

Small Corner
Notched
(Woodland)
(Northern Plains and
Rocky Mountains)

Prairie Side Notched
(Woodland)
(Central and Southern
Plains)

Plains Side Notched
(Woodland)
(Central and Southern
Plains)

Parowan
(Woodland)
(Fremont Culture)
(Colorado and Utah)

Illustration 49f

Huffaker
(Woodland)
(Great Plains)

Harrell
(Woodland)
(Rocky Mountains
and Great Plains)

Triangular Unnotched
(Woodland)
(Rocky Mountains
and Great Plains)

Washita
(Desert Side Notched)
(Woodland)
(Rocky Mountains
and Great Basin)

Reed
(Desert Side
Notched)
(Woodland)
(Rocky Mountains
and Northern Plains)

Bottom Notched
(Woodland)
(Rocky Mountains
and Great Plains)

Leaf-Shaped
(Woodland)
(Rocky Mountains
and Great Plains)

Stemmed
(Woodland)
(Rocky Mountains
and Great Plains)

Illustration 49g

CHAPTER 7

STONE ARTIFACTS

PERFORATION ARTIFACTS

The Drill

Of all the artifacts other than arrowheads, the drill is one of the more fascinating and delicate implements that can still be found today. There is some problem here in common terminology. Various archaeologists and authorities use the term *awl* interchangeably or in place of the term *drill*. The artifact that I am about to describe I prefer to call a drill; afterwards I'll describe and illustrate what I consider to be an awl.

The true drill is a finely worked and delicate, oblong tool that was often T-shaped. The drill must have broken rather easily with use, for in hunting artifacts for more than forty years, we have found only three perfect ones but have found many bases, tips, and center sections. It is my speculation that most of the perfect drills were either found many years ago or are discovered through excavation.

The drill was used primarily for drilling holes in leather, stone, or other material. Hides would then be sewn together to make shelter or clothing. Animal sinew or yucca fiber was used as thread. Most needles used were made from bone rather than stone. Drills were also used to

make holes in bone, rock, pottery, shells, and wood used in the manufacture of implements, beads, and other items.

I have seen tips of drills that were as sharp as a pin and others that
were well worn. Resharpening was a necessity with continued use of
this artifact, unless the drill broke completely, in which event it was
probably discarded. Many smaller drills were actually reworked broken
projectile points. Almost all stone drills were hafted for use with a shaft
or handle, such as shown in illustration 52.

Drills have also been known to be made of bone. Most of these
types of drills are found through supervised excavation of sites below
the surface, where they have been preserved by nature. A bone drill is
next to impossible to find on the surface due to rapid deterioration by
weather as well as through the action of mice and other rodents who
find the material to be a good source of calcium. The illustrations shown
herein depict drills made of flint materials. You will notice that the drill
was made for use either by holding in the hand or for hafting to a shaft.
Illustrations 50 and 51 show some of the types of drills that can be
found, most of which were hafted to a handle or shaft for actual use.

The Awl

The awl, as opposed to the drill, is not ordinarily found as much in
the T-shape of a common nail as is the drill and many times may be
nearly as wide as it is long. The awl was almost always held in the hand
rather than notched and hafted to a shaft. The awl, like the drill, was
principally used to make a hole in another material, such as a hide. Also,
the artifact that I consider to be an awl was ordinarily made only of flint
materials. Sometimes the awl is bifacial, or worked on both sides, but
many times it is unifacial, or worked only on one side or at the point.
Frequently the awl is domed and is not always as thin as a drill or a finely
worked arrowhead. The perfect awl seems to be more common than the
perfect drill, primarily because the drill broke more easily during usage
and while lying on the ground than did the awl. An awl is often found
in perfect condition, other than perhaps a worn or slightly broken tip.
More often than not, the awl is made with a natural indentation for the

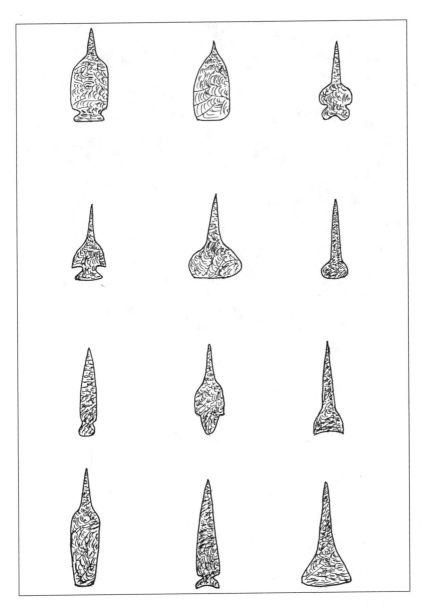

Illustration 50 Assorted stone drill styles, some of which are reworked tools and projectile points and most of which were hafted for use.

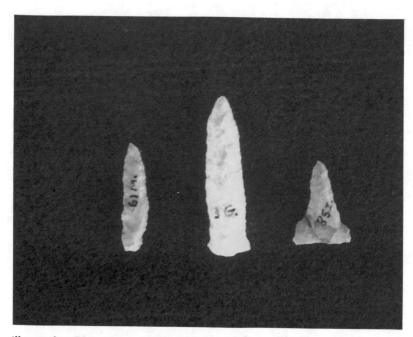

Illustration 51 Three drills from the author's family collection. The one on the right has probably been resharpened more than once.

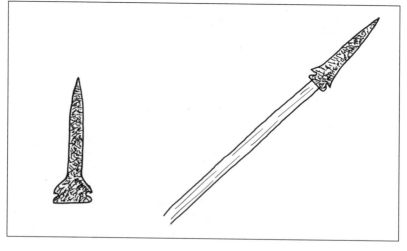

Illustration 52 Hafting of drill.

thumb or forefinger to aid in using the tool. On close examination, the awl may fit perfectly into either the right or left hand. Illustrations of some of the awls that we have found in northern Colorado and southern Wyoming follow. (See illustration 53.) Illustration 54 depicts awls that are 2 to 3 inches long and 1 to 2 inches wide at the widest point.

The Graver

The graver is an interesting stone tool that is difficult to find, at least in areas where I have hunted, but that might be common in other parts of the country. A graver is also one artifact that could be overlooked easily as just another piece of flint. It is not easily recognized in the field and must actually be picked up and closely inspected for the presence of a very small amount of workmanship. The graver is basically a small flake or piece of flint material that usually contains one small spur on one edge. Sometimes the flake will contain more than one spur, but this type is rare. The spur will generally be small and short and sometimes may reveal a very minimal amount of workmanship. Very close inspection and sometimes a good deal of speculation are required to identify gravers. Others may, on occasion, be easily recognized.

The graver was used to perforate or cut thin hides and other material much in the same manner as the awl or drill, but it was obviously not fitted for the heavier use of these tools. A sharp graver will easily split open a tough material, however. The graver was also used for incising or etching, and perhaps even for tattooing of the skin. The graver is an interesting and somewhat mysterious artifact, to say the least. The gravers shown in illustration 55 are approximately the size of a silver dollar. Two of the three gravers shown in illustration 56 were found in association with Paleo points, and many authorities feel that their use may have been more common during Paleo times.

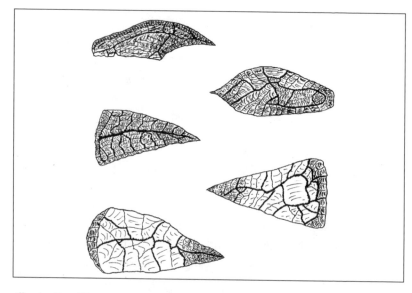

Illustration 53　Various types of awls in the author's collection found by the author's family. Illustrated by the author.

Illustration 54　Awls found by the author and his family.

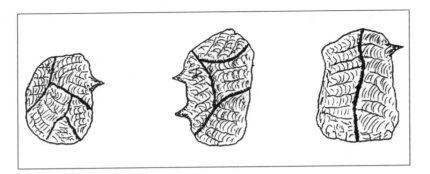

Illustration 55   Three typical types of gravers.

Illustration 56   Three gravers from the author's family collection. The two on the right were found at known Paleo sites.

SCRAPING AND CUTTING ARTIFACTS

The Scraper

Almost any good-size piece of flint material could have been used as a scraper in one way or another, and a good imagination may come in handy in trying to identify one. Actually, any sharp piece of flint material could be used as a scraper without any flintknapping at all. These artifacts are referred to as "utilized flakes" and may be very difficult to identify. Sometimes the finely worked, perfect scraper is as hard to find as the perfect arrowhead .

Scrapers range in size from those as small as a thumbnail (from which the thumb scraper takes its name) to those as large as the palm of the hand. They were used primarily in scraping hides, bones, and other similar materials in the preparation of food, weaponry, clothing, and shelter. The true scrapers, as distinguished from those that require a certain degree of speculation or imagination, are generally not hard to identify. The workmanship and shaping of the flint material, for example, is often delicate and deliberate, and at least one good scraping edge of the artifact is easily recognizable by even an inexperienced person. Generally, the scraper is worked or shaped on one side only, with the reverse side being smooth, unworked, and many times concave in shape, caused primarily by the manner in which the flint material originally fractured. The bifacial scraper is somewhat thicker than the stone knife, which can be similar in appearance but is usually quite thin when compared to a scraper. A bifacial scraper may have been, in fact, a preform. To further complicate identification, a knife could many times also be used as a scraper, for these implements were often interchangeable. I once helped skin an antelope with a knife that I first considered to be a scraper. This artifact also worked well in scraping the antelope hide after completion of the skinning process. I have since categorized the artifact as a knife, mainly because it is thin and worked on both sides.

Many times the thumb scraper in particular will have a perfect indentation for thumb placement. Also, the worked side of the scraper often has a visible "ridge" running almost the full length of the artifact, which resulted from the original fracture of the flint in the flaking process.

Scrapers are generally categorized as thumb or thumbnail scrapers, side scrapers, end scrapers, side and end scrapers, and snub-nosed scrapers, whose categorization usually depends upon the location of the worked edge on the artifact. Side and end scrapers are shown in illustration 57. The top and side views shown at the bottom of the illustration reveal the slight ridge running almost the full length of the artifact on top, caused by the original fracture of the material. In the side view, you can also see the turtleback or humpbacked characteristic of the artifact. The smaller thumb scrapers and snub-nose scrapers shown in illustration 58 have the same general characteristics as the larger scrapers in illustration 57. Most of these scrapers are no larger than a quarter or a fifty-cent piece. Illustrations 65 and 66 show the same scrapers from both the top and the bottom, or underside, view.

To find scrapers, you have to be able to recognize the smooth, concave feature of the underside of the scraper that shows no workmanship of the flint at all. For some unknown reason, this unworked side is almost always the visible side when the scraper is lying on the ground—at least this has been my experience. It may be passed over very easily as just another flake of flint unless you actually turn it over after recognizing it as a possible scraper. I have turned over many nice scrapers with my hunting stick without ever bending over. It is always a pleasant surprise to find the beautiful workmanship on the reverse side of the scraper after turning it over. Sometimes the pieces have to be picked up and examined very closely to see the delicate chipping workmanship along the edge. It would be easy to discard a scraper like this after a careless and quick examination. Always remember that rarely is there any reason to be in a hurry. Take time to study the artifact closely in the field, or at least take it home and study it further under a good light or with a magnifying glass.

Many artifact collectors do not have much regard for the scraper, perhaps because scrapers are relatively common and are not as fascinating as the arrowhead. Archaeologists, however, find the scraper to be just as interesting and valuable in their studies as the arrowhead itself. I have always maintained that I would rather find a nice scraper than a broken arrowhead. The delicate workmanship on many scrapers is indeed a fascinating work of art.

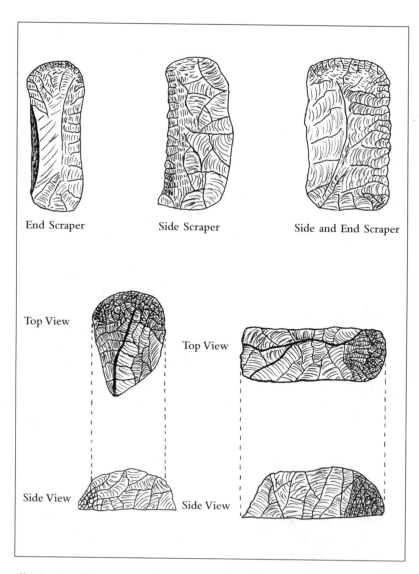

End Scraper   Side Scraper   Side and End Scraper

Top View

Top View

Side View   Side View

Illustration 57   Various types of large scrapers illustrated from the author's family collection.

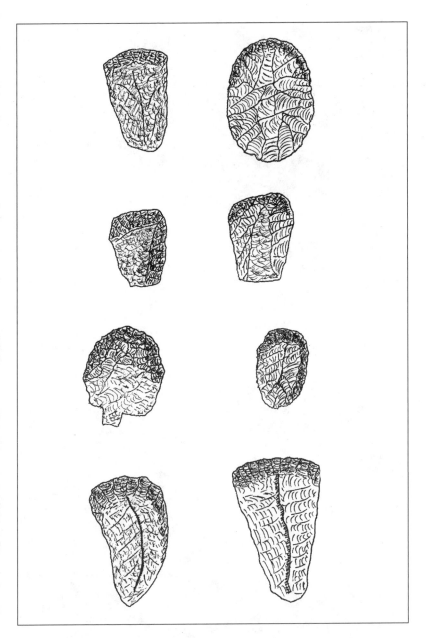

Illustration 58 Various types of smaller thumb scrapers illustrated from the author's family collection.

Illustration 59 Two large scrapers from the author's family collection. The one on the left fits very nicely in the author's left hand, as shown in illustration 60.

Illustration 60 The large scraper from illustration 59, held by the author.

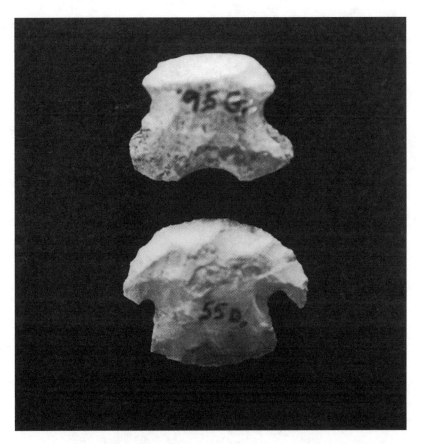

Illustration 61   Two nice hafted scrapers, both found by the author's wife in southern Wyoming.

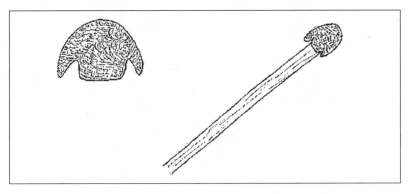

Illustration 62   Hafting of scraper.

Illustration 63 Half of a smooth Gastrolith, or stomach stone of a prehistoric fish or reptile used in the digestive process. Ancient peoples would sometimes flake or chip the underneath edge and use this stone as a scraper, as shown in illustration 64.

Illustration 64 The underneath, or worked side, of the Gastrolith in illustration 63.

Illustration 65 Assorted unifacial scrapers photographed from what could be considered the top, or worked side, of the scraper. Illustration 66 shows the same scrapers from the bottom, or unworked side, of the scraper.

Illustration 66 Bottom or unworked side of scrapers shown in illustration 65. Note the characteristic flat or concave smoothness on this side, which resulted from the natural flaking process of the flint material.

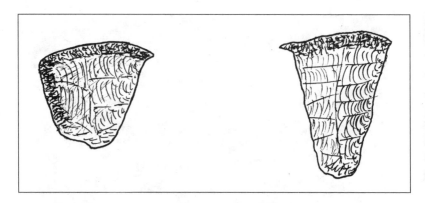

Illustration 67   Two spurred or "beaked" scrapers, which were both found in areas where Paleo points have been found. Most authorities associate this type of scraper with Paleo cultures. The spurred portion of the scraper was used to score or cut material, which made it a multipurpose stone tool.

The Knife

The flint knife is somewhat similar to the scraper, although it is generally longer, thinner, and larger than the scraper and normally is bifacial rather than unifacial. Sometimes, in fact, the flint knife will have a striking resemblance to a typical steel hunting knife, although generally it is not as long. The knife was obviously used to cut various materials such as meat, hides, wood, food products, and other fibrous materials, such as yucca.

Many knives that I have found are sharp enough to get the job done. With flint being comparable, in degree of hardness, to steel, it is easy to see why the knife was such an essential item in the prehistoric tool kit.

Most knives are simply categorized as knives, with no particular sub-categories, as with scrapers. Some, however, will have only one cutting edge, while others will have two to four cutting edges. Generally, the smaller the knife, the more cutting edges it will have, and the larger the knife, the fewer cutting edges it will have. Two knives that come to mind that have been categorized are the Tang knife and the Cody knife, shown

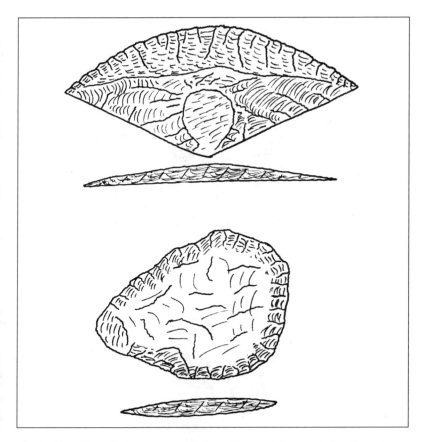

Illustration 68   Various types of knives, illustrated in actual size from the author's family collection.

in illustration 72. These knives are not found in perfect condition very often and, in my opinion, are quite rare. The Tang knife was no doubt made for hafting onto a wooden shaft—note the characteristic notches. The Cody knife was probably also hafted and used with a handle. Knives are artifacts that are very difficult to categorize without a certain amount of speculation. The utilized flake mentioned previously could easily have been used as a knife. Also, many projectile points, especially those with serrated edges, could have likewise been used as knives. Many knives

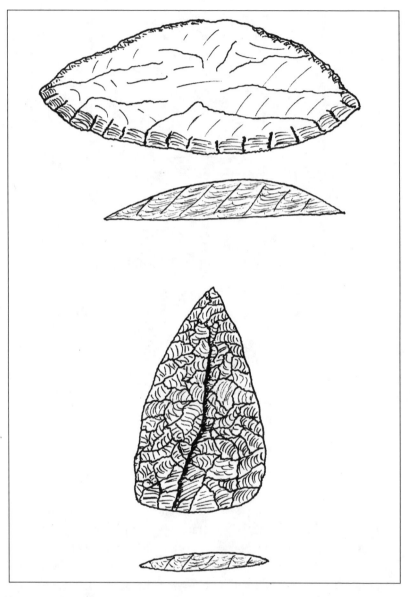

Illustration 69   Various types of knives, illustrated in actual size from the author's family collection.

Illustration 70 The larger single-edge knives from the author's family collection are shown in the top row, as compared with the smaller, multi-edge, leaf-shaped knives in the bottom row.

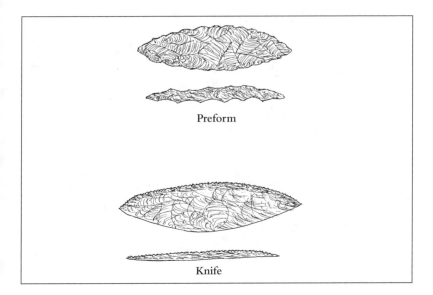

Preform

Knife

Illustration 71 This illustration shows the basic difference between the preform and the finished knife. The preform, shown at the top, shows the roughed-out edges and thickness of the stone, while the finished knife shows further bifacial thinning and a finely worked cutting edge.

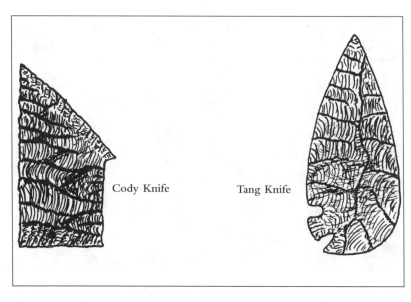

Cody Knife   Tang Knife

Illustration 72   The classic Cody and Tang knives, both made for hafting.

Illustration 73   A quarry blank (middle), a preform (left), and a finished knife (right). Note the gradual thinning, reduction in size, and finer workmanship that occurs at each stage of the flintknapping process.

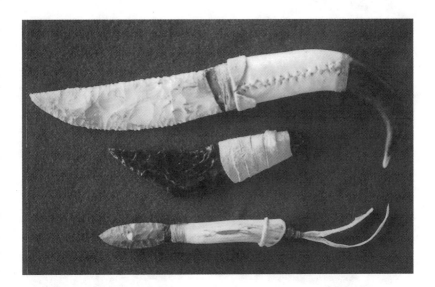

Illustration 74   Three contemporary hafted stone knives made by George Stewart, expert flintknapper, trapper, amateur archaeologist, and one of the most knowledgeable people I have met over the years. The knife at the top is hafted in an antelope horn, the one at the bottom is hafted in a bone handle, and the obsidian knife in the center is simply wrapped with rawhide.

were hafted such as those shown in illustration 74. Most of these knives were not notched like the Tang knife; they were often just inserted into the wood, bone, or horn used as the handle and wrapped with sinew or other hafting material. Sometimes a portion of the knife was simply wrapped with rawhide to serve as a protective handle.

The Blade

The blade is an oblong piece of flint material that was often bifacially thinned but not always finished as a finely worked knife. When finished as a knife, a blade would simply have to be referred to as a knife, in my opinion. Many authorities use the terms *knife* and *blade* interchangeably. The larger blade shown in illustration 75 has been referred to as a *macroblade,* while the smaller blade in the same illustration has been called a *microblade.* These blades show evidence of unifacial or

Illustration 75   The macroblade at the top compared with the microblade at the bottom.

bifacial working along one edge and will often have a ridge running the full length of the blade. This ridge has caused some authorities to refer to these blades as "prismatic" flakes because of their prismlike appearance. The prismatic flake or microblade is rarely found in the areas with which I am familiar, although they are perhaps more common in other parts of the country. The microblade shown at the bottom of the illustration is actually only 1/2 inch wide and 1 inch long.

The Chopper

Any large piece of flint material with a good edge could probably have been used as a chopper. A chopper was used to chop or cut other

Illustration 76   The chisel.

materials, just as the name implies. Generally, the chopper will lack the finely worked edge of the knife. In some cases, the chopper might have been a blank or a preform for a knife and may have simply never been finished as a knife. A chopper with a finely worked edge would have to be referred to as a knife and would more than likely have been handheld rather than hafted.

The Chisel or Gouge

The chisel could also be easily mistaken for a knife or scraper. Its use, however, was probably not for scraping or cutting, as with the scraper and knife, but rather for gouging or chipping, as with the modern cold chisel used in woodworking. In fact, with a bit of imagination, it does resemble the modern cold chisel, although it is usually somewhat shorter in length. (See illustration 76.)

The Saw

The flint saw is also similar to the knife, but it is distinguishable primarily because its cutting edge is much more coarse or serrated than the finely worked knife edge. In effect, it does resemble the typical handheld modern ripsaw blade. The only stone saw that I have found is approximately 4 to 5 inches long with one roughly serrated cutting edge. It was definitely sharp enough to cut most any material. (See illustration 77.)

Illustration 77   The saw.

The Crescent

The crescent is a very fascinating and rare stone artifact in the cutting category. Some archaeologists believe that the crescent is found only in and about sites that contain prehistoric Paleo points. This may well be true, because the only one I have found was in an area where I had previously found a classical Folsom point, in eastern Colorado. Interestingly enough, the flint material was exactly the same material as the Folsom point.

The crescent can be either concave or convex and many times is also quarter-moon in appearance, with one sharply worked cutting edge drawing to a point on one end. The crescent is usually made of good quality flint material such as jasper or chalcedony. (See illustration 78.) A somewhat larger crescent, perhaps 5 or 6 inches long, has been found in California to a limited extent and has been termed the Stockton curve. As far as I know, this particular form of the crescent is extremely rare. In any event, the crescent was used as a knife and was probably handheld or hafted.

The All-Purpose Tool

The all-purpose tool is a rare stone artifact that would logically fit into the perforating, cutting, and scraping categories. Its use as a grind-

Illustration 78   The crescent.

ing tool is unlikely. This artifact is normally larger than a thumb scraper or a drill but smaller than a large knife. The all-purpose tool always has one end worked to a point for perforation, with the opposite end worked in the form of an end scraper. One side is worked rather delicately for use as a knife. It is almost always oblong in shape and generally fits either the right or left hand quite well. Illustration 79 shows the versatility of this stone artifact. This artifact can be difficult to distinguish from the awl, as the two are similar in shape.

The Adze

Another cutting artifact very similar to and hard to distinguish from the chisel is an adze. The adze was generally longer and wider than the chisel and was many times shaped like an axe blade. The adze was made from hematite and from the flint materials by both percussion and pressure-flaking techniques. It was, like the chisel, used in woodworking and can vary anywhere from 2 to 8 inches in length. The adze normally has one flat side, with the opposite side somewhat convex in nature. (See illustration 80.)

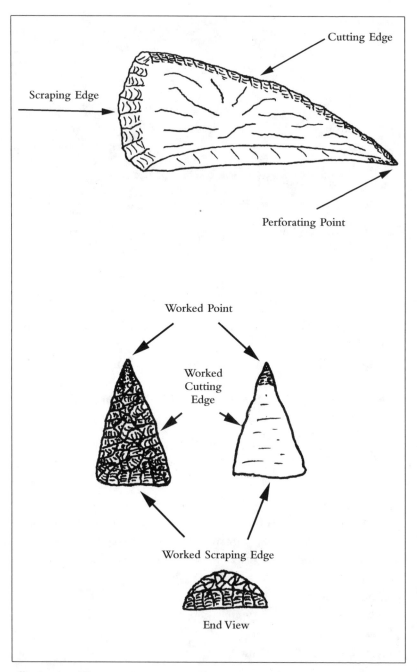

Illustration 79   The basic construction and uses of the all-purpose tool, illustrated in actual size from the author's family collection.

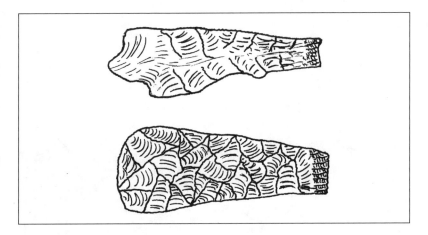

Illustration 80   The adze.

The Burin

The burin is a stone tool that may be classified as a cutting implement similar to the chisel, adze, and graver. Like the graver, it was used primarily as a scoring, cutting, or engraving tool, and yet, in appearance, it more closely resembles the chisel or adze. It was probably smaller than the adze, and it is hard to differentiate from a small chisel. Generally, one end (the incising end) will be finely worked by pressure flaking. (See illustration 81.) Illustration 82 shows a comparison of what I believe to be a narrow knife, a wide drill, and an adze or burin, in that order from left to right. Note the similarity in appearance of the artifacts.

The Axe

The stone axe is an interesting forerunner of the modern-day axe used primarily for chopping wood or other course materials. Very few of these artifacts are made of the flint materials, and most of them were shaped by pecking and grinding of rock such as granite, hematite, basalt, slate, iron ore, and occasionally sandstone or limestone. Normally the stone axe is one of the larger stone artifacts; it can range from one to

Illustration 81   The burin.

Illustration 82   These three artifacts, included for comparison, are categorized by the author as a knife, drill, and adze, from left to right.

twenty pounds in weight. This artifact is usually grooved for hafting
onto a wooden handle. The grooved axe shown in illustration 83 is actually better depicted in illustration 84. It may be distinguished from the
maul or hammerstone by the sharp edge, as compared to the rounded
or blunt end of the maul or hammerstone. The hand axes shown in illustration 85 are basically the same artifact without the grooved feature.
In many parts of the country, the hand axe is also referred to as a celt.
Generally, the top and bottom edges of the hand axe or celt will be

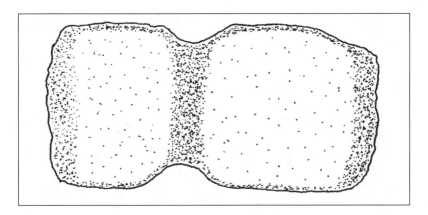

Illustration 83 The typical stone axe, illustrated.

Illustration 84 Grooved axes, which were found in Wyoming.

Illustration 85   Two typical hand axes or celts.

rounded and smoothed in order to be more comfortable for handheld use. Grooved axes and celts seem to be far more common in the eastern rather than the western United States. The upper Midwest seems to have an abundance of these stone artifacts, probably because trees and other vegetation are more numerous than in the arid plains regions.

Spokeshaves or Shaft Scrapers

The spokeshave is an interesting and somewhat rare stone artifact. It is usually made from the flint materials and can be easily mistaken for a flake of flint material. Normally the spokeshave is about the size of a small scraper and can be distinguished by having one or more indentations on the sides. It is thought that this stone tool was used to shave or scrape down the wooden arrows or spearshafts in order to get a more perfectly rounded arrow or spear for better flight. Much of the wood used for arrows was not perfectly round because of small twigs,

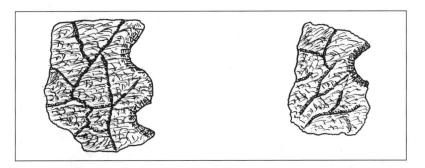

Illustration 86   Spokeshaves or shaft scrapers.

Illustration 87   Spokeshaves or shaft scrapers from the author's family collection.

nodules, and bends. The spokeshave was used much like the old draw knife was in removing bark from a log. The spokeshave is shown in illustration number 86. Illustration 87 shows spokeshaves from the author's personal collection.

GRINDING AND POUNDING ARTIFACTS
Mano and Metate

The mano and metate are generally described as a unit since they were normally used together in grinding. The mano, otherwise known as a milling or grinding stone, could have been used alone in grinding, but the metate was generally used together with the mano. The metate, or grinding slab as it is commonly known, was just as its name implies—a stone slab used as a grinding platform. The handheld mano or grinding stone was moved back and forth or in a circular fashion on the surface of the slab to grind food or other materials from a coarse substance into a finer substance. (See the bottom of illustration 88.) Illustration 89 shows a mano on a metate that is not grooved or worn down by mano movement back and forth, but rather in an uneven or circular manner.

The grinding stone was hardly ever made from flint material, probably because of the hardness of flint and the sharp edges left as a result of the conchoidal fracturing. A far more suitable stone for grinding was a smooth, well-worn river rock, such as granite or sandstone. A smooth rock was more comfortable to the palm of the hand and could probably have been used for several hours with little discomfort.

Most grinding stones are 4 to 6 inches long, 3 to 4 inches wide, and 2 to 3 inches thick—usually somewhat larger than a clenched fist and oblong or round in shape. Generally both sides of the stone have been flattened through heavy usage upon the grinding slab, although many times a stone will only have one side flattened. Many grinding stones when flattened on both sides will resemble a new bar of soap. Illustration 88 also shows, at the top, the various forms of manos that can be found according to wear or use patterns.

The grinding stone is a common find in the northern Colorado foothills and the plains of eastern Colorado, partly because these areas were more heavily populated throughout the year than the higher mountain elevations. Also, many substances that were ground were only found at lower elevations. On the other hand, the grinding stone

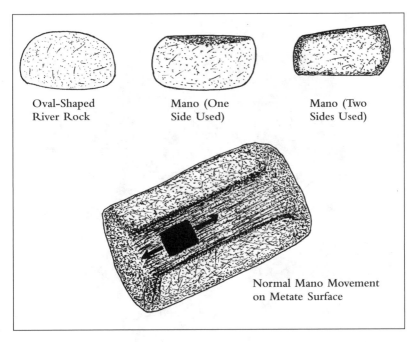

Oval-Shaped
River Rock

Mano (One
Side Used)

Mano (Two
Sides Used)

Normal Mano Movement
on Metate Surface

Illustration 88   Variations of the mano, or grinding stone, showing degrees
of wear, from the original smooth river rock to flattening of both sides. At the
bottom, the normal use of the mano on the metate, or grinding slab,
is illustrated.

can be found in the higher mountain elevations where berries and
seeds grew wild and were ground in food preparation.

Over the years, I have found several grinding stones on open and
steep ridge areas above campsites. This has led me to conclude that
they were also used to prepare hides for clothing and shelter. Many that
I have found were in close association with scrapers of all sizes and
types in areas above campsites. Although it is possible that food could
have been ground in the high areas above campsites, it seems more logical that hides would have been scraped, smoothed, and prepared for
clothing and shelter in open areas away from the campsite itself.

Although the grinding stone is commonly found, it is not always
easy to find. Many times it may appear on the surface as just another

Illustration 89   A mano and metate both made from granite.

rock until it is turned over to reveal the flattened grinding surface. Any smooth or round river rock should at least be turned over and examined, especially in an area that is a good distance from the nearest creek or river. It may be "foreign" to the area and may well be a grinding stone left by humans rather than by nature. Illustration 91 shows the natural top side of a grinding stone, once probably a river rock. It does not appear to be an artifact at all. Illustration 92, however, shows the bottom side of the same stone flattened and worn down considerably through use as a grinding stone. Again, any foreign rock of this type, especially in a known campsite, should be turned over and inspected.

The whole metate, or grinding slab, on the other hand, is very rare and difficult to find on the surface. My theory is that the grinding slab was usually large—really one of the largest stone artifacts that can be found—and because of this, the majority of the surface metates were

Illustration 90 A mano and metate both made from sandstone.

probably found many years ago. Also, there still may be several that were turned over in the campsites and that now appear as ordinary rock slabs. I believe that when early peoples temporarily left a campsite, they would simply turn the metates over so that the implements would not collect rainwater and snowmelt and then freeze and break. Upon return to the campsite, they could then simply turn over the metates and use them again. They were generally too heavy for transportation, often weighing from twenty-five to seventy-five pounds. Farmers on the Colorado plains will occasionally plow up a whole metate in a field, but most seem to be found during archaeological excavation.

The metate generally is 12 to 18 inches wide, 18 to 24 inches long, and 2 to 4 inches thick, and, of course, is flat in overall appearance. The majority of the time the metate will have a hollowed out or depressed appearance usually on one surface only, caused by the grinding and sliding movement of the mano back and forth. The metate will likewise not ordinarily be made of flint material, but rather from granite

Illustration 91   The top, or smooth, natural side of a river rock. Compare this with illustration 92, which shows the bottom, or worn side, of the same river rock.

Illustration 92   Worn side or bottom of river rock shown in illustration 91.

Illustration 93   Assortment of manos. The two on the left also show evidence of being used as hammerstones.

or sometimes a sandstone or sandstonelike material. Certain volcanic materials were also used for both metates and manos.

Many times at a campsite, several broken manos and metate pieces may be found scattered over an entire site. This material is generally referred to as *camprock*. The presence of camprock almost always indicates the location of a campsite where other artifacts may also be found. Illustration 93 shows an assortment of various manos or grinding stones that we have found over the years. Note how similar they are.

Hammerstone or Percussor

The hammerstone or percussor is similar to the grinding stone in appearance, size, and material used. Many times river rocks were also

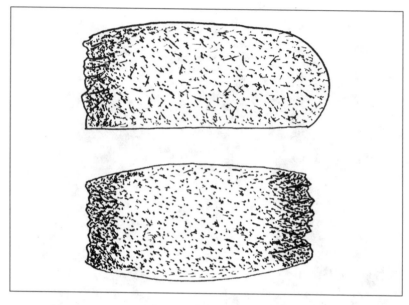

Illustration 94   The hammerstone or percussor.

used as hammerstones, probably because of their smooth surface, which would have been more comfortable to the hand. The hammerstone, as compared with the maul, was used in the hand only and was not grooved for hafting onto a wood handle, as was the maul. Other than this, the artifacts are very similar in usage and appearance. Sometimes, in fact, a mano was also used as a hammerstone, in which event, the ends of the stone, rather than being smooth, will have a broken or chipped appearance. The hammerstone was generally used in breaking larger pieces of flint material into smaller flakes and spalls to be used for arrowheads, scrapers, and the like. This was normally accomplished by either direct percussion (one stone against the other) or by indirect percussion, such as an antler being held in the hand as an intermediate tool between the hammerstone and the larger flint material. See the hammerstone or percussor in illustration 94.

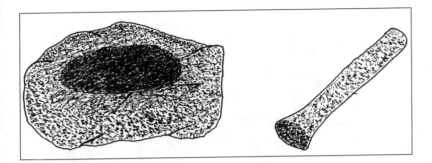

Illustration 95   Mortar and pestle.

Mortar and Pestle

Another set of grinding artifacts that seem to be rare in northern Colorado and southern Wyoming are the mortar and pestle. They may be more common in other parts of the country, such as the Southwest. This is understandable, since much prehistoric art comes out of the Southwest, and the mortar and pestle were commonly used to grind substances for painting pictographs and pottery. In this respect, pottery sherds are also relatively rare in northern Colorado and southern Wyoming. This may be because pottery was not made or used as much in the higher elevations as it was in the Southwest or lower elevations. Furthermore, pottery deteriorates much more readily in the harsher climates and simply is not commonly found except for very small pieces. The mortar and pestle were also used in grinding food substances, such as seeds, berries, and nuts, as well as medicinal herbs.

The mortar and pestle were generally made from sandstone, granite, or similar materials and were not ordinarily made from the flint materials. The mortar was usually about the size of a small bowl and, in fact, looks much like a small cereal bowl. The depression area in the center will be hollowed out and smooth from the circular grinding of the pestle. The pestle is oblong and may be somewhat larger on the grinding end as compared with the handheld end. The pestle is also made from sandstone or granite or other similar materials. The mortar

Illustration 96   A unique stone mortar found in western Nebraska.

Illustration 97   A boulder mortar discovered on a private ranch in New Mexico. The pestle was found in one of the three mortar holes. Note the presence of the metate.

and pestle are shown in illustrations 95 and 96. In some parts of the country, particularly the Southwest, many large boulders may be found that contain worn indentations such as those shown in illustration 97. These are known as boulder mortars, and they are sometimes found with pestles left in the indentations or holes. Similarly, boulder metates have also been discovered where grinding with a mano has flattened areas of the surface.

Abrader or Shaft Straightener

Another interesting stone artifact is the abrader, sometimes called a shaft straightener. This implement was often used to straighten shafts upon which the projectile point was attached on one end. The shafts themselves were usually made from branches of the wild cherry, birch, ash, chokecherry, or willow trees when these trees were available, because their wood was harder and more durable. Many times, of course, the branches were not perfectly straight and contained a number of knots where smaller twigs and branches had been removed. The shaft straightener was used to grind or smooth out the shaft and correct these imperfections. The tool itself was normally made of abrasive material, such as sandstone, when available. Other rock was used on occasion, but generally not any of the flint materials. Most abraders are somewhat small—perhaps 2 to 4 inches wide, 6 to 8 inches long, and 1 to 2 inches thick. They will always have at least one and sometimes two grooves running lengthwise or crosswise on at least one surface. These grooves, of course, are formed by sliding the material back and forth across the surface. They become deeper with increased usage. Abraders were also used to sharpen other stone tools or to grind or smooth down edges on tools and projectile points that were to be hafted. They were commonly used in the flintknapping process itself. The small, triangular abrader shown in illustration 100 was used for sharpening bone awls and needles. The abrader clearly had many uses other than shaft straightening. As strange as it may seem, these artifacts are not common in my part of the country, although they are common elsewhere. I have

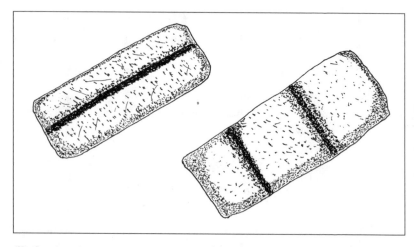

Illustration 98   Abrader or shaft straightener.

Illustration 99   Three abraders that were found in South Dakota and given to the author.

Illustration 100   Two abraders, which show the variation in size. The small, triangular abrader was most likely used to sharpen bone awls and needles.

found only one artifact that may have been used as a shaft straightener, and it is questionable.

Maul or Hammer

The stone maul can be thought of as the forerunner of the modern sledgehammer, for it is very similar in appearance. It can be distinguished from the hammerstone in that the hammerstone was typically held in the hand and used without a handle. The maul was grooved for hafting, just as the axe was used with a wooden handle. It can be distinguished from the axe by its rounded or blunt end as compared with the sharper edge of the stone axe. Similarly, the maul was also made by pecking and grinding of river rock, as flint material was rarely used. The maul can also weigh anywhere from one to twenty pounds. (See illustration 101.)

Illustration 101   The maul or hammer.

MISCELLANEOUS UTILITY ARTIFACTS
Hoe

The stone hoe may be thought of as the forerunner of the modern garden hoe, as it was used primarily in farming or gardening by prehistoric people. For this reason, it is rarely found in the higher mountain campsites where agriculture was not generally practiced. The hoe is normally found in lowland and prairie campsites where agriculture was generally practiced. It is usually a well-chipped artifact made of the flint materials, generally thinner than the axe and maul and approximately 5 inches wide and 10 inches long. It was usually notched or grooved for hafting onto a wooden handle or was sometimes hafted without the aid of notches or grooves. Many are smooth and shiny or polished due to heavy usage in the soil. (See illustration 102.)

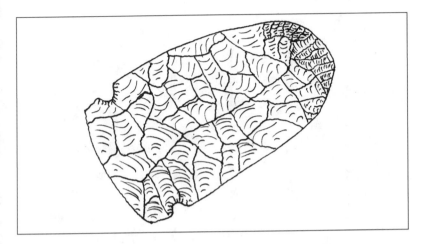

Illustration 102   The stone hoe.

Stone Balls

Round stone balls of all sizes are a common find in and about ancient campsites. Many theories have been expounded as to the exact use of these artifacts, and some people may frown at any speculation that they are even artifacts. They are common, however, in campsites, and, in my opinion, enough evidence exists of their usage that their presence is more than coincidental. They do not seem to be a popular artifact in collections, probably because they all essentially look alike, except sometimes for size.

Most stone balls are made by pecking and polishing, rather than chipping of flint materials. Igneous rock and sandstone were generally used in making the stone ball. Stone balls can generally be classified as game stones, cooking stones, hot stones, and ceremonial stones.

There is some evidence of their use as game or ceremonial stones, and it is easy to speculate that they may have been used by children in playing games or, because of their shape, used in ceremonial rituals. Good evidence exists for their use as cooking stones and hot stones. This evidence is primarily the fire-blackened color of many of these stone balls. When a rock is heated for a long time, or several times, it

Illustration 103   Assortment of round stones, from the small, pea-size stone to the larger, baseball-size stone. The round, dark area on the larger ball indicates the portion that was exposed aboveground at the time of discovery.

will develop this fire-blackened appearance. Stone balls may have been heated as cooking stones and placed in water or perhaps in stews in order to convey heat. Also, stone balls may have been laid on top of red hot coals, and then meat laid on top of the stone balls to cook. Where stone balls are found in areas containing blackened rock and ash or charcoal, and especially in a known campsite, good evidence exists that the stone ball was used in cooking. In fact, the ones I have found were fire-blackened and found in exactly this type of an area. Their use in cooking seems unquestionable to me.

It has also been said that stone balls were similarly heated and used as hot stones at hide-working sites. They were placed on the hides while red hot and used to burn or scorch off undesirable materials.

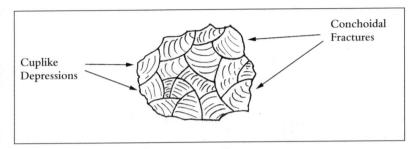

Illustration 104   The core or mother stone from which flakes were struck, leaving the characteristic cuplike depressions of the conchoidal fractures. In aactual size, this stone could be as large as a grapefruit or as small as a golf ball.

Most of the stone balls that I have found are about the size of a golf ball, although many are both smaller and larger. My theory is that the golf ball–size stones were used in cooking; the smaller ones used for games, such as marbles; and the larger ones perhaps used in ceremonies as well as games. Some have been found as large as bowling balls and may have, in fact, been used as such. Illustration 103 shows several of these round balls, the size ranging from the size of a baseball to the size of a pea.

Core

The core, to many collectors, is a very uninteresting artifact, but to the archaeologist, both amateur and professional, it is quite the opposite. The core is the larger piece of flint material from which, through percussion flaking, both direct and indirect, the smaller flakes and spalls were struck and eventually shaped into arrowheads, drills, scrapers, and the like. Stone material was actually transported great distances, especially when it was good quality material desirable for making the more delicate tools. Most of the cores that I have found were in stone quarries, campsites, and high lookout points on ridges where a person could have easily made blanks and preforms while on watch duty for the camp. They come in all sizes, shapes, and colors; most that I have

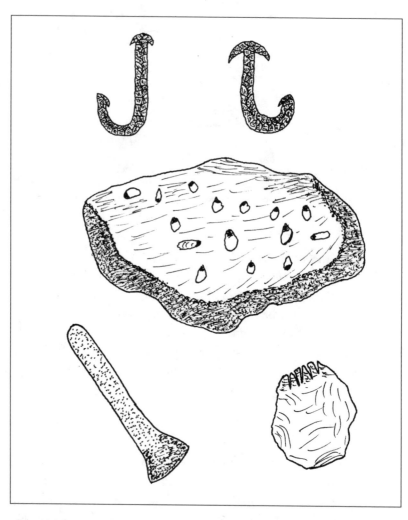

Illustration 105 At the top, two typical flint fishhooks are shown. In the center, the cup stone is illustrated to show the numerous small indentations on the top of the larger stone. The spatulate, or spud, is illustrated at the bottom left, and the sinewstone is at the bottom right.

found are the size of a baseball or somewhat larger. Illustration 104 shows the core after a number of smaller flakes and spalls have been struck from the stone, leaving the cuplike conchoidal fractures.

Fishhook

I have heard several knowledgeable and well-informed people question whether stone fishhooks were ever made or used by prehistoric cultures. Others seem to take for granted the fact that they were commonly used. I simply don't know who is right.

The stone fishhook, if made at all, was normally made of the flint materials and is a rare find, especially in areas where little fishing was done. In the northern Colorado mountains, where many beaver ponds exist, a person could have probably caught more fish by hand rather than going to the trouble of making and using a fishhook. Many stone fishhooks have supposedly been found in the coastal regions and in areas of the country that have large rivers and lakes. (See illustration 105.)

Moccasin Last

The moccasin last is another very questionable stone artifact. Some people seem to take for granted that they were made and used, while others almost scoff at the notion that they are artifacts at all.

The moccasin last, if used at all, was used to shape leather for footwear. I can recall seeing only one in an artifact collection myself, and it could have easily been a geofact or shaped by nature rather than a human. As one might expect, the moccasin last is shaped like a human foot.

Rubbing Stone

The rubbing stone is a stone artifact commonly mistaken for the average small river rock, for it is usually very smooth and shiny and generally no larger than the palm of the hand. This artifact could very easily have initially come from a riverbed before being carried to a

Illustration 106   Assorted ceremonial or ornamental stone artifacts are illustrated as follows: top row on the left, bannerstone; top row on the right, birdstone; second row from the top on the left, boatstone; second row from the top on the right, dome or cone; center row on the left, bird effigy; center row on the right, turtle effigy; second row from the bottom on the left, charmstone; second row from the bottom on the right, spool; bottom row, both right and left, two examples of stone pipes.

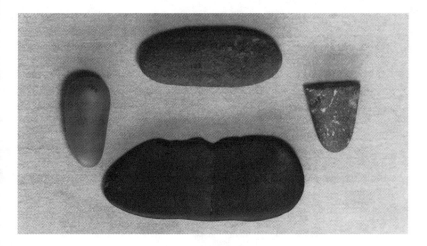

Illustration 107   Assorted rubbing or polishing stones.

campsite. It is commonly a stone such as granite or a river rock such as that used for a grinding stone or mano. The rubbing stone was used in rubbing hides used for clothing and shelter and in smoothing pottery in the pottery-making process. Its use in grinding herbs and small food materials also cannot be ruled out. It is hard to imagine other possible uses except for perhaps ceremonial purposes. The rubbing stone would probably not be recognized as a stone artifact anywhere but in a campsite location. When one is found in a campsite out of its natural location, it is obvious to me that it was transported to the site for a purpose. I might add that rubbing stones are commonly found in campsites, which is probably not a mere coincidence. A sampling of various rubbing stones can be seen in illustration 107.

Whetstone

The whetstone is an unusual stone artifact that is relatively rare, particularly in the Rocky Mountain region with which I am most familiar. It was used as an abrader to sharpen other tools simply by rubbing back and forth. These stones are usually less than 6 inches long and are typically cylindrical in shape so that they fit well in one hand.

They usually have a very smooth or polished surface from heavy usage, and only through the visible signs of heavy use can you really determine that a stone is, in fact, an artifact. Almost any stone material could have been used for a whetstone, and no one material in particular seems to have been used more commonly. A whetstone is shown in illustration 143 in the bottom left-hand corner.

Cup Stone, Cups, Paint Bowls

These three types of stone artifact have been grouped together because they were, in fact, very similarly used by prehistoric cultures. The cup stone has been described by some authorities as being a larger, slablike stone perhaps more than a foot in diameter with several small, cuplike indentations on the surface of one or both sides. These indentations were used as mortars to hold nuts and various other substances that had to be finely ground or broken apart for usage. Normally, a pestle was used to accomplish the breaking or grinding of the substances. I have never personally seen one of these artifacts, and I would suspect that they are somewhat rare.

On the other hand, individual paint bowls or cups have been found that were readily identifiable as stone artifacts. Any naturally hollowed-out stone material could have been used for a bowl or cup, and some appear to have been hollowed out by pecking or grinding. A cup or bowl can be truly identified as a stone artifact if it is discolored by the various substances that it contained. Certain herbs, berries, or minerals very clearly left permanent, stained discoloration in bowls or cups. For example, minerals, vegetation, and berries were mixed with animal fat and other substances to make the various paints used by prehistoric people. These substances, when mixed and finely ground over and over in the same container, will leave a permanent discoloration clearly different from the natural stone color. In this regard, the minerals iron oxide ore and red ochre were used, leaving a red color; copper ore was used, leaving a green color; and charcoal was used, leaving a black coloration. A small bowl is pictured in illustration 143 in the upper right-hand corner. The cup stone is shown as the large item in the center of illustration 105.

Spatulates or Spuds

The spatulate or spud has been recognized and categorized by some archaeological authorities as a flared celt. It was ordinarily 8 to 10 inches long with a smooth, slender handle and was typically flared out at the base or on the cutting edge. My research indicates that it was ordinarily made from the flint materials by percussion, grinding, and polishing. It was used somewhat like a chisel or knife in dressing hides and debarking trees. Some authorities believe that it may also have been used as a ceremonial object. The spatulate is shown in illustration 105 on the lower left-hand side.

Sinewstone

The sinewstone seems to be a very rare stone artifact, and I have personally never seen one. It is usually rather small, in order to be held in one hand, and may have several incised lines or indentations on one edge where sinew material was drawn back and forth to prepare the material for use as bow strings, thread, or string for fastening or hafting stone tools and projectile points onto a wooden shaft. Probably any stone material could have been used for the sinewstone, although it would seem that a softer material such as soapstone or slate, or an abrasive material such as sandstone, would have been more appropriately used. The sinewstone is shown in illustration 105 on the lower right-hand side.

Atlatl Weights

As stated previously, the atlatl was a device used by prehistoric people to propel or throw a spear before the age of the bow and arrow. Simply stated, the atlatl was usually a rather short, wooden-handle-type device, as shown in illustration 40, in which the spear was placed and then slung or thrown toward the intended object. A stone weight was often used in conjunction with the device to add velocity, stability, and balance to the throw and also to make the device more controllable and accurate. This stone weight, or atlatl weight, was typically made by grinding, polishing, and pecking techniques employed on slate, fireclay, soapstone, siltstone, catlinite, or other similar stones. The stones often contained one or more drilled holes used for fastening. These weights were ordinarily rather small and were often winged, grooved, and barrel shaped. Bannerstones, birdstones, and boatstones explained in the next section as ornamental or ceremonial stone artifacts are thought by many archaeological authorities to have been primarily used as atlatl weights. These are shown toward the top of illustration 106.

CEREMONIAL AND ORNAMENTAL ARTIFACTS

Effigy

The effigy is a very interesting artifact usually made of stone. It is also rare and hard to find. Effigies are normally made of slate, soapstone, pipestone (or catlinite), or the usual flint materials. They are made by pressure flaking in the case of the flint materials, and by grinding and polishing of the other softer stone materials. The classic thunderbird or eagle is perhaps the more common effigy, but stone effigies of other birds, turtles, fish, lizards, snakes, geese, and trees have also been found. The only practical use of such effigies has always been considered to be ceremonial or ornamental. Two examples of effigies are shown in illustration 106.

Pendant

The pendant is an artifact that sometimes was made of sandstone, soapstone, catlinite, or basalt. In certain locations, it was made of pottery, shell, bone, hematite, or slate. It was generally ornamental and most often worn as a necklace. The pendant can be almost any size or shape but is generally not too large and is quite similar to modern-day jewelry. The pendant may have also been used in ceremonials. It can be distinguished from the amulet and gorget, for it generally has only one small hole drilled entirely through the material, rather than two holes. (See illustration 108.) Some pendants are found as blanks, or pendants never drilled, such as the two shown in illustration 109.

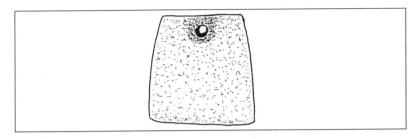

Illustration 108   The pendant.

Illustration 109   Assorted pendants and pendant blanks made from pottery, sandstone, basalt, bone, and shell. The pendant blanks at the top were found by the author and his wife. All the drilled pendants were found by Garry Weinmeister, a very capable and knowledgeable amateur archaeologist from Windsor, Colorado.

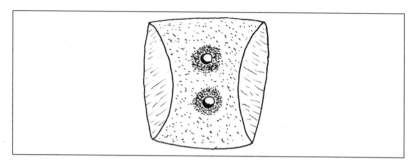

Illustration 110   The gorget.

Gorget

The gorget is another scarce artifact. I have never found one and can only recall seeing pictures of them or reading about them. The gorget is usually thin and flat, concave on one side and convex on the other, and generally has two holes drilled completely through the stone (usually basalt, hematite, or slate). There are four general theories regarding its use: (1) it was fastened to the left forearm to protect against the slap of the bowstring upon shooting an arrow; (2) it was worn ornamentally around the neck; (3) it was used as an object around which to twist twine; and (4) it was used as a shuttle in weaving. (See illustration 110.)

Amulet

The amulet is yet another comparatively rare artifact, at least in my area of the country. I have never found one or ever seen one found. It is usually cigar shaped with a hole perforated through each end. Most amulets are made of slate, hematite, greenstone, or quartz, and some have grooves around the body rather than holes. They may have had the same uses as the gorget. They are, however, generally thicker and longer than the gorget. Also, some think that the amulet may have been the forerunner of the modern string or bolo tie. (See illustration 111.)

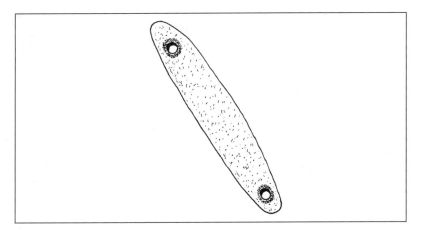

Illustration 111   The amulet.

Discoidal or Disc

The discoidal, commonly called a disc, is a stone artifact that is more common in the north-central United States. I have never seen one in a collection in my part of the country, nor have I found one. It is circular in shape and concave on both sides. Quartz or granite was a common material used for this artifact, although some have been found made from standard flint materials, hematite, slate, or basalt. They range from 1 to 9 inches in diameter and from one to twenty pounds in weight. Some have been found with a hole perforated through the center and others simply with flanges around the edges. Many discoidals show very little abuse and seem to have been well cared for, which leads to the theory that they were used for ritual or ceremonial purposes. Others believe that they were used as small bowls for mixing herbs and seeds to make medicines. (See illustration 112.)

Plummet

The plummet is an interesting stone artifact that resembles a carpenter's plumb bob. It is usually made from basalt, slate, or hematite. It is rare; I have never found one nor personally seen one in a collection. The plummet may be several different sizes and shapes but is

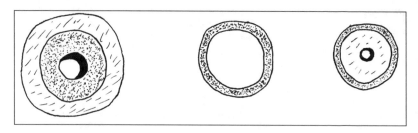

Illustration 112   The discoidal or disc.

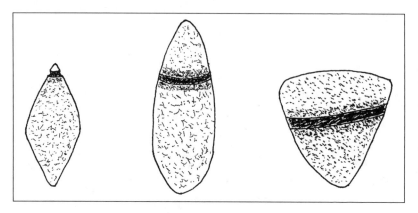

Illustration 113   The plummet.

characteristically marked by a single groove around it toward one end or the middle. Some archaeologists believe that the plummet was used as a sinker for fishing, while others claim that it was a ceremonial or ritual stone, perhaps used in curing the sick or in bringing rain. Still others believe that it was used as a bola stone or worn as a pendant around the neck. The plummet is shown in illustration 113.

Beads

Most beads were made from shells, bone, pearls, metals, seeds, teeth, wood, and pottery. Beads were also made from stone, although not exclusively from the flint materials. Any small and pretty stone could be worked into use as a bead, although my research has shown

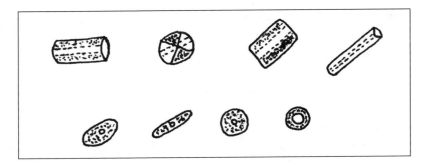

Illustration 114   Various bead styles.

that stone beads are rare when compared to beads of other materials. With the intrusion of early settlers, glass beads were traded for and thereby came into common usage. Beads, of course, were primarily ornamental. Beads can be found in almost any size or shape but are usually circular, cylindrical, or ovular in form, and they are almost always perforated for easier stringing. Although beads are widely found throughout the country, I have never had much luck in finding any. Many people claim to have found beads in anthills, probably in the area of a campsite. Some of the general sizes and shapes of beads are shown in illustration 114.

Stone Pipes

Another interesting and unique artifact is the stone pipe, whose use is surrounded by various legends and theories. While the pipe is not commonly found in the Rocky Mountain area, it is found regularly in other parts of the country, particularly in the Midwest and northern central plains areas. Pipes were made from a number of different materials, including clay, bone, and wood, but perhaps the most unique source material was catlinite, more commonly known as "pipestone."

Pipestone is a unique material found primarily in one area of the United States. Pipestone National Monument has been established by the U.S. government in a small area of southwestern Minnesota, where this material is found in abundance in natural quarries. In fact, some authorities believe that almost all of the catlinite used in making pipes originated in these quarries—it appears to be the only sizeable deposit of catlinite in the entire country. Pipestone itself is specially suited to carving and fashioning into a pipe, and while making a pipe was by no means easy, this material was probably more easily worked than any other. It would probably be extremely difficult to make a pipe out of any of the flint materials. Catlinite is red in its natural color and is soft when compared to most stone material. In this regard, I would think that pipestone is probably best compared to what is commonly known as "soapstone" or steatite, a soft gray material similar in geological composition. Soapstone is still used today to make various ornaments and figures, perhaps also including pipe bowls.

Sometimes only the pipe bowl itself is made out of pipestone, while the pipe stem is made from bone or wood. However, some stone pipes are made entirely from pipestone. In the ordinary manufacturing of the pipestone pipe bowl, a flint knife was used to cut and "rough out" the bowl itself. A wooden shaft with an attached stone drill likely made of flint material was used to hollow out the bowl. Scrapers or abraders were then used to polish and smooth down the rough edges.

While catlinite can be purchased today in its natural state and also in the form of various ornaments, including pipe bowls, I am not aware of any location where it can simply be found. It is illegal, of course, to pick it up in Pipestone National Monument. It would appear that outside of the legal purchase of pipestone, the only other way you could obtain a pipestone pipe would be to find one on an artifact-hunting excursion on private land. While this might be easy in some parts of the country, it would be extremely difficult in the Rocky Mountain area. Two examples of stone pipes are depicted at the bottom of illustration 106.

Bannerstone, Birdstone, and Boatstone

These three types of stone artifact have been grouped together because of their similarity, not only in construction but also as either ceremonial or ornamental artifacts or atlatl weights. These implements were typically made from slate, catlinite, or similar soft materials, usually by pecking, grinding, and polishing. Often they were drilled with one or more holes perforated entirely through the material. While the birdstone is typically shaped in the form of a sitting or nesting bird and the boat-stone is generally a hollowed-out shape like a small boat or canoe, the bannerstone is usually barrel shaped or winged in appearance. Almost all of these artifacts are small and, depending upon the archaeological authority, were used either as ceremonial and ornamental artifacts or, because of their size and construction, were used as atlatl weights. All three artifacts are very rare outside of the Mississippi Valley and north-central United States, including the entire Great Lakes region. The winged, butterfly design of the bannerstone is one of the most highly treasured artifacts anyone could have in a collection. Three general designs of these artifacts are shown toward the top of illustration 106.

Cone or Dome, Charmstone, Spool, and Quartz Crystal

The cone or dome is a stone artifact usually made from granite or hematite by pecking and polishing. It is normally small and can be held in one hand. The base is flat with the top pointed or domed—thus the name cone or dome. Its use is speculated to be ceremonial, although not much is really known about the artifact.

The charmstone was also probably used as a ceremonial piece, with any other use being unlikely. It is generally cylindrical, being somewhat smaller at each end, and it may be a few inches in length. Sometimes the charmstone is drilled or perforated. Ordinarily it is made from hematite or granite by pecking and polishing. As with so many of the other ceremonial stone artifacts, it is unusually rare and not found in many artifact collections.

The spool is exactly as the word implies. It is an ordinary spool made from stone, more often sandstone, with a hole perforated lengthwise through the center. Its use was likely ornamental or ceremonial in nature, although an artifact of this type could have easily been used in games. It, too, is extremely rare and not found in many artifact collections. The cone, charmstone, and spool are shown in illustration 106.

The quartz crystal is a puzzling but rather common find in campsites, and its use seems to have been either ceremonial or ornamental. It is difficult to imagine any other use. Actually, it is hard to categorize the quartz crystal as an artifact at all unless it is found in a known campsite. I have personally found several in campsites and have always thought that they had some particular significance to prehistoric cultures. My experiences with finding the crystal are not unusual; in fact, some authorities report several instances similar to mine and claim that such quartz crystals were used for ceremonial or ornamental purposes. A quartz crystal that I found in a campsite is shown in illustration 143, second from the left side in the middle row.

CHAPTER 8

WHERE ARTIFACTS ARE FOUND

To find arrowheads and stone artifacts, you obviously have to know where to look. You can literally walk for miles and hours and never even find a piece of flint, much less an artifact, unless you have some idea of where you ought to be looking.

A basic understanding of the prehistoric cultures and habitats of your area is a must in order to zero in on productive areas. A good, thorough study of the prehistoric lifestyle will give you a better idea of where these people lived, hunted, and generally spent most of their time. As an example, some were hunter-gatherers and frequented many places, and some were of an agricultural society and pretty much stayed in one area. There are, of course, many books available on this subject.

Archaeological sites can be classified into a number of different categories depending upon the location and nature of prehistoric activity of early cultures as well as the ordinary forces of nature occurring since the time of the activities. The following are some of the major references used when referring to archaeological sites.

CAMPSITES

The most common is probably the ordinary campsite, or the place where prehistoric people lived. Looking for a campsite can be a very interesting and also very frustrating experience. Assuming that you have a basic knowledge of the prehistoric culture and habitat of your area, some campsites are readily recognizable. The classic campsite, at least in the foothills of Colorado, is on a rather high plateau facing or sloping to the east, south, or southeast with a few scattered pine trees and a source of water, such as a stream, spring, or lake, within a short distance. Quite often a spring is found within the campsite itself, feeding a stream or lake lying below to the south or east. This campsite is a typical non-agricultural site. The people here depended upon hunting and gathering, rather than the growing of crops, for their food supply. This is a permanent campsite, rather than seasonal, especially if found in the lower foothills as opposed to the higher mountains. If this same campsite were found in the high mountains, it would more likely be a seasonal site.

The site will ordinarily be located on a south or east slope, such as the site shown in illustration 116, because of its proximity to the sun in both winter and summer. Also, a south or east slope usually is much more protected from the north and west winds that prevail on the southern Wyoming plains and in the northern Colorado foothills. Oftentimes the study of wind patterns in your area will be quite helpful in locating campsites. In some areas the campsites may be located on southwest slopes, for instance, because of prevailing winds. The main campsite in illustration 116 is located near the center of the picture on top of the bluffs and down the slope to the right. I have found very few foothill campsites that were directly exposed to a strong northwest wind. The site is usually located on a high point, such as a small plateau or shelf, or on a ridge with an excellent view in at least three and sometimes all four directions. A typical campsite of this kind can be seen in illustration 117. An elevated campsite provided protection from floodwaters and a safe, broad view of the surrounding country. A high site was also easier to defend against an enemy and, of course, helped minimize the chances of a surprise attack.

Illustration 115   A typical old western homestead that was also the location of a prehistoric campsite because of the topography and presence of water nearby.

Illustration 116   A typical river-bluff campsite, with the actual site shown above the bluffs at the top and down the southeast slope to the right.

Illustration 117   A typical bluff or plateau campsite, located on the high flat area in the center of the photograph, which lies on the south end of the ridge to the right.

Aside from directional and elevational location, it was essential that a source of water be in the immediate vicinity. In the Colorado foothills, this was ordinarily a spring rather than a lake or stream. The spring usually fed a river or creek somewhere nearby, or at least a natural lake in the general area. In looking for a campsite, be careful to distinguish between the natural and the man-made lake or pond, for it is essential to view an area as it would have existed hundreds of years ago. The dry lake-bed site shown in illustration 118 lies entirely around the dark area in the center of the picture. The dark area was once a natural lake and is clearly indicated by the topography of the area and the darker vegetation and soil in the low area. Even today there is probably a greater than normal accumulation of subsurface moisture in the former lake bed.

Illustration 119, on the other hand, shows a typical campsite located on bluffs above a present lake with the creek flowing into it. In this regard, many springs that may have been excellent sources of water several hundred years ago may now be dry and difficult to identify. The

Illustration 118   The campsite shown lies entirely around the darker vegetation and dirt area in the center, which is a dry lake bed showing evidence today of subsurface moisture only. The main campsite is located on a south slope above the dry lake.

same is true with dry creek beds, although they are usually easier to locate than dry springs due to the terrain. You need to be somewhat familiar with vegetation and its growth in an area once occupied by water. Even though a former spring may now be dry and have no surface water, many times subsurface moisture will still be present and thereby give the area a greener appearance than the surrounding area. A stand of buffalo grass, for instance, may be heavier in a particular area than in the immediate vicinity. Furthermore, many springs, even today, will dry up in drought years and flow during wet years, so you must constantly observe the area for hidden signs. A typical campsite located at a spring is shown in illustration 120. Of course, many good, large springs still exist that probably look no different than they did hundreds of years ago. These will be obvious, and many times campsites will be found in the immediate vicinity.

Illustration 119 The campsite shown in this photograph is in the foreground on a small plateau above the lake. The bluffs behind the lake also contain similar small campsite locations.

Illustration 120 This campsite, at a spring, lies entirely around the spring in all directions, on both the higher and lower ground.

Illustration 121   When the water level is down, many stone artifacts can be found on sandbars and gravel bars, as in the river channel shown here. These artifacts are almost always out of archaeological context, and extra precaution must be taken because of the surrounding environment, which may include snakes and quicksand.

Sometimes ranchers have converted natural springs into small stock-watering ponds, so a campsite might be found by what appears to be a man-made lake as opposed to a natural lake. Here again, you must study the area carefully.

Aside from topographical characteristics, the primary indicator of a campsite is the presence of flint chips either heavily or lightly dispersed through the area. In this regard, you should always check out any anthills in the area. An anthill in a campsite will contain thousands of small chips of flint material about the size of a pinhead. Anthills may also contain beads. You must be careful, however, to distinguish between flint material that has been chipped, flaked, or "worked" as opposed to a natural outcropping. The campsite will, upon close inspection, have literally hundreds of very small chips present, the small size due to the delicate pressure-flaking technique. Others, of course, will be larger, having resulted from percussion flaking. More often than not, the larger cores or "mother stones," some as large as a volleyball, may be present. Naturally, if the campsite is heavily hunted or perhaps "hunted out," the amount of flint and, indeed, the number of artifacts present, will be reduced considerably. Even then, an area such as this will yield broken arrowheads and scrapers provided the hunter has enough time and patience to look for them.

In any campsite location, you will usually find more bases of arrowheads than tips. You may also find many whole arrowheads that appear to be perfect but that upon close examination will reveal the very fine needle point to be missing. The reason for this appears obvious to me. The prehistoric hunter, no doubt, came back to camp from hunting with broken arrowheads attached to arrows that had been shot. He probably just detached the bases and broken arrowheads and reattached newly made points to the arrows. Likewise, the broken tips of arrowheads are usually found as stray finds in hunting areas where they were shot and broken off upon impact. Broken tips found in campsites probably resulted from accidental breaking during the original arrowhead-making process. Similarly, many perfect arrowheads can be found in campsite locations perhaps because they were never used in the first place, or they were simply left behind. Every now and then, a completely perfect arrowhead can be found as a stray find in hunting areas. In this event, I think that the arrow was shot and either lost or simply never retrieved for further use.

Another indicator of a campsite is the presence of the so-called tepee ring, as shown in illustrations 122 and 123. Archaeologists have focused much discussion and debate on the "tepee ring" over the years. Some have concluded that tepee rings were used for exactly the purpose the name implies; others say that they were ceremonial stone circles and had nothing to do with the tepee. In any event, the presence of circles made from stones is not natural and does indicate the presence of prehistoric activity one way or another. The rings usually vary from 6 feet to 20 or 30 feet in diameter. Ordinarily, the stones are underground with only the tops exposed on the surface. This is probably caused by wind or surface water runoff over many years on relatively

Illustration 122   A small tepee ring on a lightly traveled road, which I actually drove through before I recognized it as a tepee ring.

Illustration 123   A typical larger tepee ring, or perhaps a ceremonial stone circle, well disguised by nature.

level ground. The rings are generally found on somewhat level ground as opposed to steeper slopes. Most of the stones themselves are the size of a volleyball or basketball and may be side by side or even several feet apart. Some rings are difficult to distinguish because some of the stones are completely covered up by dirt or perhaps moved out of the original circle by humans or animals. I have rarely found artifacts in or near tepee rings. I have seen several tepee rings in the general locality of campsites, however, and I believe that the rings were often used for ceremonial purposes in addition to holding down the edges of tepees.

My experience has revealed that another common indication of a campsite is the presence of yucca plants growing naturally and freely in an area. I have seen a great number of campsites with yucca plants growing in abundance throughout the entire site. A study of prehistoric cultures reveals that this is not really a coincidence. Prehistoric people used the entire yucca plant for many purposes, such as food, clothing, footwear, baskets, and even soap. Due to its remarkable number of uses, the yucca plant was no doubt a true necessity.

Another indicator of a campsite is the presence of a hearth or pit. Generally, the hearth and pit were used to build cooking fires and fires used for warmth in cold weather. Occasionally, the pit was used for campsite waste materials. The pit was ordinarily deeper in the ground than the hearth, but both the hearth and pit were generally lined with stone. In either case, the soil in the location of a hearth or pit often is discolored—either black soil from charcoal remnants or fire-blackened soil and rocks caused by intense heat. Both the pit and the hearth were usually circular, thereby causing discoloration in the earth in a circular pattern. Therefore, if you encounter a darkened circle of earth, it will most certainly be evidence of a campsite. Once again, if any excavation is done, it should be left to the professional archaeologist, who can accomplish such a task under proper field conditions.

The presence of piñon trees is another good indicator of a campsite. Prehistoric cultures used the piñon nut as food, and because of this, almost every natural grove of piñon pines will have a campsite located nearby.

Illustration 124   A typical hilltop or knoll site on the prairie, located on the top of the high area in the center of the photograph.

On the eastern Colorado and southern Wyoming plains, the campsite ordinarily is found on high knolls and generally not too far from sources of water. A typical knoll site on the plains is shown in illustration 124. Knolls along creek beds are usually good areas for campsites in just about any part of the United States.

HUNTING GROUNDS AND KILL SITES

Many archaeological sites throughout the country will be found in areas that are not located on high ground nor near water. These sites may not have been habitation sites, or so-called campsites, but rather hunting grounds, also sometimes referred to as kill sites. Hunting grounds and kill sites can be found most anywhere and, of course, many times are on high ground or near springs and other water sources. The main distinguishing feature between the hunting ground and the campsite is the absence of a concentration of many small flint chips. Often pieces of flint material found in hunting grounds are usually pieces of artifacts as opposed to mere chips. A kill site, on the other hand, may contain small chips of flint material resulting from resharpening of knives or other stone tools. The primary determination that must be made is whether the flint material has been "worked." To do this, you must look for the characteristic conchoidal fracture that exists as a pattern, rather than by accidental chipping or breaking. Most specimens found in hunting areas will have been worked, while this is not necessarily true in campsites.

Furthermore, some knowledge of game-animal behavior and habitat will help considerably in discovering hunting areas. Deer, for instance, will travel the higher ridges in the Colorado foothills, while antelope on the plains will many times stay in draws or low-lying areas, probably for protection from high winds. Game animals will also habitually use established game trails in the foothills. Deer, for example, will often cross a ridge in a "saddle" or cut. Also, game animals in the northern Colorado foothills frequently occupy the high eastern slopes of the many "hogbacks." The high eastern slopes are generally covered with more vegetation than those on the west, which often drop straight off as cliffs. Many arrowheads can be found as "stray finds" on the hogback hunting grounds. In addition, arrowheads can frequently be found in low-lying hunting grounds along, and actually in, riverbeds, in places generally too low for campsites.

BLOW-OUT SITES

In the Great Plains and many other areas, especially in the West, where much sandy native soil still exists, over the years the wind has created areas known as "blow-outs," such as that shown in illustration 125. Most, but not all, of these blow-outs are on the prairies where the lighter, sandy soil is more common. This type of soil is moved more easily by the wind, especially when dry weather conditions exist. Blow-outs can range from a few feet to hundreds of feet in diameter.

Illustration 125   A typical blow-out site, shown in the entire area of the photograph around the lighter sandy soil.

Some large blow-outs result in what are called parabolic sand dunes. After a strong wind with little associated moisture, a wide variety of artifacts may be uncovered and easily spotted from several feet away lying alone on the hardpan after the sand has blown away. Vegetation in these areas is usually rather sparse, and any foreign material stands out noticeably. Some blow-outs have been created by farmers through plowing. In extremely dry, windy climates, careless soil conservation is not always the cause of these "man-made" blow-outs. Sometimes they simply cannot be avoided, and they probably would have become natural blow-outs in a matter of years anyway. Keep in mind that all natural blow-outs probably started as normal land before the effects of wind erosion became evident. Perhaps modern humans have simply aided the natural erosion process in some instances. On the other hand, the modern farming method known as "no-till" farming, where the ground is plowed infrequently, has undoubtedly diminished the presence of blow-outs considerably. Likewise, the vast amount of land that has been placed in the governmental Conservation Reserve Program, commonly called CRP Land, has also reduced the number of farm acres under cultivation. This land is usually planted in tall grass and naturally prevents blow-outs from occurring. Many acres of good artifact-hunting grounds have been taken away from the arrowhead hunter by these modern soil-conservation methods.

In any event, blow-outs are typically good places to hunt artifacts wherever they occur. I have never really decided whether the artifacts in blow-outs came from campsites on the location or whether they were generally stray finds. I suspect that in most cases where a large amount of flint or small flint chips are found in the area, the site was probably a campsite at one time, whereas in areas where flint is scarce, the artifacts are probably stray finds resulting from hunting.

Finally, in hunting any blow-out or even a blown area of a field, the better hunting will generally be on the side from which the wind has blown through the area. Usually the ground on this side will be blown clean, exposing the hardpan and many more rocks, while on the opposite side of the blow-out, sand will have accumulated, perhaps covering up rocks and artifacts. The blow-out has to be closely studied prior to hunting after the most recent windstorm. Wind, of course, can and will vary from time to time, and on a future trip to the area, the opposite side of the blow-out may be blown clean.

GAME ENTRAPMENT, BUFFALO JUMP, AND WALLOW SITES

Another site worth mentioning is the "buffalo jump," which is occasionally found at the base of a rather high cliff or precipice. Such a hunting or kill site is shown in illustration 126. Buffalo were driven to the edge of a cliff to the point where they eventually pushed one another over the side. The buffalo were then killed or butchered at the base of the cliff. Many artifacts other than arrowheads have been found in these processing sites; knives and scrapers may be more

Illustration 126   A buffalo jump or game entrapment site, shown in the center of the photograph and below the cliffs.

prevalent. Although much has been said and written about the so-called buffalo jump sites, I have personally known of very few and suspect that they are not as numerous as commonly thought to be. A similar site, shown in illustration 127, is the buffalo wallow, where buffalo gathered because of the presence of water, mud, or moisture. These sites are normally hunting or kill sites, although they may have also once been campsites. The actual site shown in the illustration is the dark area in the center foreground just below the long snow bank. In dry weather when moisture was scarce, these wallows were used by buffalo as "dust wallows," so it is obvious that buffalo probably always frequented these areas.

Some experts feel that buffalo were more often herded or driven into deep arroyos (deep gullies) and then killed at the upper end where the steep side walls prevented their escape. Any area containing arroyos will also normally contain at least some artifacts on the surface. Since these areas are subject to frequent erosion, a good many of the artifacts have probably been buried for many years.

Illustration 127   The buffalo wallow site shown in the center of the photograph and below the snowbank is in the darker soil, which was heavily soaked with what appears to be perpetual moisture in an area between two springs.

QUARRY SITES

Another common site is the quarry site, which is ordinarily found near natural outcroppings of flint material. These areas are commonly found throughout the entire United States. Flint materials that are native to an area are usually located toward the tops of the ridges in natural outcroppings. Occasionally you will find an artifact at one of these sites, but more often than not, very little of the flint material will be worked. Larger pieces were normally broken down first into what are called quarry blanks and then perhaps worked into preforms, more suitable for transportation. In this respect, a thorough search of the area should be made, because a campsite may be in the immediate vicinity. Prehistoric people ordinarily did not transport heavy rock any farther than necessary unless the material was unique and of a fine quality. Even then, it was probably transported as quarry blanks or preforms rather than rough, large pieces of flint material.

LOOKOUT SITES

The lookout site can be easily confused with the quarry site, especially with a natural outcropping of flint nearby. A person on a high lookout would often make arrowheads and other artifacts to pass the time. The lookout site will obviously be located on a high area and can be distinguished from the quarry site by the presence of many more smaller-size flakes and chips of flint resulting from pressure flaking. Percussion flaking was ordinarily used at the quarry site, and the pieces of flint material remaining will normally be larger than those left at the lookout site.

CEREMONIAL SITES

The ceremonial site, in my opinion, is characterized by the presence of "tepee rings," some as large as 40 feet in diameter. These sites will usually be located not far from a campsite and generally on higher ground, although I have occasionally seen this type of site on lower ground. It has also been my experience that artifacts in ceremonial sites are rare, but some authorities would probably dispute this finding. A ceremonial site can be easily distinguished from a campsite or quarry site because of the lack of many large or small chips or flakes of flint material.

PLOWED FIELDS

Plowed farm fields, especially when located along rivers, have always been good places to find arrowheads and other stone artifacts. This is true not only in the river valleys of the West, but throughout the entire country, probably more so in the eastern United States. In my opinion, this is true because these areas often were the locations of campsites. Prehistoric people lived near water and in agricultural areas, and these locations were more suitable for growing crops. The same is still true today. Generally, it will be difficult to find artifacts in a plowed field until a good rain washes down the newly plowed dirt and exposes rocks—many times camprock or other flint material. When first unearthed by the plow or other tillage farm equipment, a rock will be covered with dirt and hard to see. Once washed by rain, however, the artifact will literally stand out in the surrounding soil.

Plowed fields exist in naturally irrigated areas such as in the Midwest and eastern United States, where annual rainfall is greater. They also exist in the West in river valleys that are irrigated with river water by farmers and ranchers. Plowed fields likewise are found in the many dryland farm areas of the United States. When hunting dryland farm ground, the same principles of hunting generally apply. The main difference, of course, may be the lack of a river nearby. Campsites in these areas are generally located on higher ground and often close to natural lake beds or springs. I have seen many areas of dryland farming where almost every high area in a field held evidence of prehistoric activity. On occasion, these dryland farm fields will also contain blowouts. Many times the blow-out areas are located on the higher areas of a field, which are naturally more subject to wind erosion.

RIVERBED AND CREEK BED SITES

A surprising number of stone artifacts are found in riverbeds and creek beds throughout the entire United States. When hunting in these areas, a person must be extra cautious to obtain permission from the adjoining landowners on both sides of the river or creek. Many times these areas are owned by federal, state, or local governments, so the removal of artifacts may be illegal. Most artifacts found in riverbeds have been deposited there by floodwaters or as a result of riverbanks caving in during periods of high water. These artifacts are almost all out of their original archaeological or stratigraphic context. Most of the stone artifacts were probably a result of hunting activities or campsites that existed along the rivers. When hunting these areas, always check the sand or gravel bars in the river; this is where most artifacts are found, although occasionally some may be found directly in the water. Small artifacts will often be found in sandbars, while larger artifacts are normally found in the gravel bars. An artifact will "hang up" in material that is comparable in size to the artifact. See illustration 121.

LAKES AND SEASHORES

Prehistoric people frequented lakes and seashores just as people today do. Stone artifacts have often been found around lakes and many times in the lakebed itself below the high water line. Most of these artifacts resulted from camping and hunting activities in these areas during prehistoric times. Even today it is not unusual to find grooved axes and hammers in the larger stones around a lake. This is especially true in the upper Midwest areas of this country. Again, proper permission should be obtained to hunt these artifacts on privately owned land. Many recreational lakes throughout the country are owned by federal, state, or local governments, where any removal of stone artifacts is illegal.

Likewise, arrowheads and stone artifacts are commonly found along the seashores around the United States. Prehistoric activity was quite common along all of the coasts, because this is where much hunting and habitation occurred. Beach erosion over many years has exposed archaeological sites and continues to do so today. Most of the stone artifacts found along the seashores are out of archaeological context because of beach erosion. Like with lakeshores, caution must be taken in hunting artifacts along beaches because many of these areas are owned by federal, state, and local governments, and the removal of stone artifacts is illegal. A person must be sure a beach is privately owned and have the proper permission to hunt stone artifacts.

COMMON CHARACTERISTICS

One characteristic that seems common to many artifact sites is a location on high ground in comparison to the surrounding terrain. This is not always true, however, for one of the finest campsites I ever hunted is located on a wide-open, low-lying area with several surrounding hills and ridges. The presence of an excellent spring and pond is perhaps the main reason why many different prehistoric cultures used this site for literally thousands of years. Folsom points have been found at this site, together with newer projectile points of Archaic or Woodland cultures. This site, for that matter, is without question the most productive one I have ever hunted. As an example of how artifacts will "work up" or "weather out" of the ground, I found part of a Folsom point at this site in the early 1960s, and fifteen years later, my daughter found another portion of the same point in the same general area. Given enough years, we may eventually find the entire Folsom point.

Another good place to hunt for artifacts is around a promontory point, such as the rock outcropping in the center of the prairie land shown in illustration 128. Such outcroppings seem to have attracted prehistoric people, perhaps for protection against the elements in camping, or perhaps as a hiding place to help in hunting game animals. Such locations are not always on high ground, and, in fact, many are located in rather low areas. In any case, even one lone, unusual outcropping in the middle of a flat plain may very well have one or more artifacts in the surrounding area.

Outside of the few exceptions described previously, high ground is the more likely location for many sites. I have seen areas in eastern Colorado where every high knoll on the relatively level terrain was literally covered with flint material. Also, remember that the arrowhead featured on the frontispiece was found in the middle of Greeley, Colorado, on what used to be known as Petrikin's Hill. This high knoll is now occupied by the student center of the University of Northern Colorado. Likewise, the highest part of Longmont, Colorado, known as Sunset Hill, was once a prehistoric campsite but is now occupied by a golf course and swimming pool. Pioneers of the area found several arrowheads on the hill when it still existed as native soil. These are only two examples; there are, no doubt, many more such former sites on higher ground in cities and towns now covered by asphalt, grass, and cement that will never again yield an artifact.

Illustration 128   The campsite shown here entirely circled the promontory point, or rock outcropping, standing alone on the prairie. Note also the remains of a homesteader's ranch buildings around the base of the rock formation. A natural lake exists to the right of the rock formation, which is not featured in the photograph.

Early cultures probably camped often on the higher banks of streams and creeks. Early fur trappers described such camps in the Rocky Mountain region in later writings and journals. I suspect, however, that many artifacts found in creek beds and along the low-lying areas around rivers resulted from hunting rather than camping activities. Game animals frequented these areas in years gone by, and, of course, rivers are still considered to be good hunting areas today because of the presence of water. Similarly, old-timers have described finding many arrowheads and other stone artifacts in the low valley areas of both Carter Lake and Horsetooth Reservoir in the northern Colorado foothills back in the early 1900s before either reservoir was constructed. These areas, now owned by the government and totally covered with water, were probably once very good hunting grounds and campsite areas.

It has been said than an arrowhead or artifact can be found anywhere, and I suspect that this may be true. I have heard of arrowheads being found in gravel driveways, the gravel having been transported from gravel pits along rivers in the area. Similarly, I heard that an arrowhead was dug out of the asphalt in a Fort Collins, Colorado, city street—again probably originally carried in with the gravel from a river in the area. Other such stories are common, so I always look for artifacts wherever I am. You just never know when or where one may turn up.

Before we leave the subject, it is important to mention the best way to familiarize yourself with the general area you plan to hunt both before and during your trip. United States Geological Survey quadrangle maps, as shown in illustration 129, are excellent for studying the topography and terrain of a given area. If you are not totally familiar with an area, they may even keep you from getting lost while hunting, for almost every dirt road and trail is shown, including many that would not be shown on an ordinary road map. Variation in elevation, including mountain tops and drainage areas, are shown together with natural and man-made landmarks, such as springs, windmills, wells, mines, lakes, quarries, and rivers. Each map covers only a given area, known as a quadrangle. Some maps may actually cover more than one quadrangle in more isolated areas. Each map will be named in accordance with a well-known landmark in the area. Sometimes you can study one of these maps before a trip and actually pinpoint several possible artifact sites without ever having seen the terrain itself. These maps and a symbol chart, such as that shown in illustration 130, are available from various U.S. Geological Survey offices throughout the country and also at certain bookstores, outdoor stores, and real estate offices.

The best way to locate a site is to be fortunate enough to have someone show you or tell you where one is. You may find a site pretty well hunted out in this manner, but in future years, after erosive forces

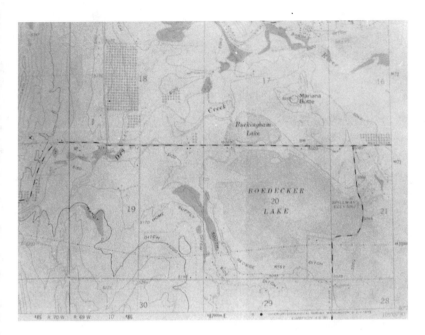

Illustration 129   U.S. Geological Survey map, or quadrangle map.

have affected the surface, many new artifacts may eventually show up. The arrowhead hunter's dream, of course, is to walk upon a site, perhaps in an isolated area, that no one has hunted for many years. These sites seem few and far between, and you may have to walk for miles and even wait for many years to discover one. I have personally run across very few sites such as this, but the possibility is always there. This is what keeps you walking over "just one more ridge" in search of the elusive artifact.

TOPOGRAPHIC MAP SYMBOLS

Primary highway, hard surface

Secondary highway, hard surface

Light-duty road, hard or improved surface

Unimproved road

Trail

Railroad: single track

Railroad: multiple track

Bridge

Drawbridge

Tunnel

Footbridge

Overpass—Underpass

Power transmission line with located tower

Landmark line (labeled as to type) .... *TELEPHONE*

Dam with lock

Canal with lock

Large dam

Small dam: masonry — earth

Buildings (dwelling, place of employment, etc.)

School—Church—Cemeteries .... Cem

Buildings (barn, warehouse, etc.)

Tanks; oil, water, etc. (labeled only if water) .... Water Tank

Wells other than water (labeled as to type) .... o Oil .... o Gas

U.S. mineral or location monument — Prospect .... ▲ x

Quarry — Gravel pit .... ⚒ .... ⚒

Mine shaft—Tunnel or cave entrance .... ⚏ .... Y

Campsite — Picnic area

Located or landmark object—Windmill .... ○ .... ⚑

Exposed wreck

Rock or coral reef

Foreshore flat

Rock: bare or awash .... * .... ✸

Horizontal control station .... △

Vertical control station .... BM ✕671 .... ✕672

Road fork — Section corner with elevation .... ₊429 .... ₊58

Checked spot elevation .... ✕ 5970

Unchecked spot elevation .... ✕ 5970

20

Illustration 130a   Geological Survey map symbol chart.

Boundary: national ....

State ....

county, parish, municipio ....

civil township, precinct, town, barrio ....

incorporated city, village, town, hamlet ....

reservation, national or state ....

small park, cemetery, airport, etc. ....

land grant ....

Township or range line, U.S. land survey ....

Section line, U.S. land survey ....

Township line, not U.S. land survey ....

Section line, not U.S. land survey ....

Fence line or field line ....

Section corner: found—indicated ....

Boundary monument: land grant—other ....

Index contour	Intermediate contour .
Supplementary cont.	Depression contours ..
Cut — Fill	Levee ....
Mine dump	Large wash ....
Dune area	Tailings pond ....
Sand area	Distorted surface ....
Tailings	Gravel beach ....
Glacier	Intermittent streams ..
Perennial streams	Aqueduct tunnel ....
Water well—Spring ..	Falls ....
Rapids	Intermittent lake ......
Channel	Small wash ....
Sounding—Depth curve.	Marsh (swamp) ....
Dry lake bed	Land subject to controlled inundation
Woodland	Mangrove ....
Submerged marsh ..	Scrub ....
Orchard	Wooded marsh ....
Vineyard	Bldg. omission area ...

21

Illustration 130b

CHAPTER 9

HOW TO HUNT ARTIFACTS

Once you know what to look for and where to look, it helps considerably to know how to hunt stone artifacts. Every artifact collector has his or her own style and method of hunting artifacts. Those that follow are my own and have proven productive over a period of forty years.

In my part of the country, I tend to hunt the lower elevations less than 7,000 feet from October to April while rattlesnakes are in hibernation. I have encountered very few rattlesnakes in summer hunting at lower elevations, but the possibility is always present. When you have to concentrate on trying to avoid rattlesnakes, it seriously breaks the concentration required to find artifacts. I would prefer not to have to worry about rattlesnakes at all. During the snake season, therefore, I hunt from April to October in the higher elevations above 7,000 feet. Hunting the higher elevations during these months also seems to coincide with more favorable weather conditions at higher elevations in the summer and lower elevations in the winter. Also, as long as snow does not completely cover the ground, it is possible to hunt artifacts throughout the winter at lower elevations.

I also have a pattern of hunting various sites at certain times of the year. Some sites are good enough that a yearly visit will yield several new artifacts on the surface that have weathered up from rains and winds over the past year. Sometimes after a hard summer cloudburst a site may have several new artifacts washed up, and good hunting may exist several times a year. Sites this good, however, are rare. The constant forces of erosion have to be taken into account wherever you are looking for artifacts.

Artifacts will work up to the surface in most seasonal areas of the country through heaving of the soil caused by intermittent freezing and thawing. In sandy or sandy loam soil areas, most artifacts will work up through heavy winds blowing the topsoil. In many areas of the country that have predominantly clay soils or hard rocky ground, most artifacts will work up due to heavy rains washing an area clean. Wind does not move much of the topsoil in this type of area and therefore plays a very small role in weathering up artifacts. On the other hand, water will erode topsoil in sandy plains areas as much as wind, especially in areas that are not level. It pays to be aware of recent weather conditions in the area you plan to hunt. Illustrations 131 through 136 show various arrowheads in situ, which have been uncovered either by wind or rain. Note the texture of the surrounding ground in each photograph.

I like to hunt in direct sunlight, preferably walking into the sun. This way I do not cast a shadow ahead of myself; an artifact is much harder to spot in a shadow. Walking into the sun will actually cause an artifact to be visible from up to 30 feet away. In this regard, I never hunt artifacts while wearing sunglasses, since they take away the shine of the flint material. I have found far more artifacts around midday with the sun high overhead than in the early morning or later afternoon hours, when the angle of the sun is such that strange shadows are cast by vegetation, including the smallest clumps of grass. I generally look for shiny, colorful stone or material that seems to be out of place or "foreign" to the area. I also have a tendency to look for white stone, because a good portion of the arrowheads found throughout the United States seem to be white or near white in color.

Illustration 131 The serrated arrowhead to the left of center was uncovered by a rain in a heavy clay soil in a dry lake bed.

Illustration 132 The white arrowhead here was exposed by strong winds blowing a light loam soil in a dryland wheat field.

Illustration 133 The arrowhead in the lower center was uncovered by rain washing through grass on a native soil almost totally covered by granite in the northern Colorado foothills.

Illustration 134 Arrowhead exposed by water in a rocky creekbed. Note the similarity in size of the arrowhead and most other rocks that surround it.

Illustration 135 The arrowhead to the left of center was uncovered by wind blowing a light sandy soil in an area of sparse vegetation.

Illustration 136 The arrowhead to the left and below center (at the right side of the larger rock) was deposited in a rocky riverbed by water flow. Again, note the similarity in size of the arrowhead and the surrounding rocks.

While walking over an area, there are certain features, both natural and unnatural, to look for. I have found a great number of artifacts in man-made dirt roads and trails made by livestock and game animals. These areas are normally barren and, of course, are subject to constant wearing away of the soil by forces other than nature. Many of these roads and trails will pass right through campsites, and flint material will be much more readily visible than in the surrounding rougher, grassy terrain. You can walk easier and travel faster on these roads and trails, and your chances of discovering a site are just as good as when simply meandering through an area.

In this connection, any area that has been pulverized by livestock is worth examining. Livestock will bed down for the night in protected areas such as where a prehistoric campsite may have been located in years gone by. Livestock will also frequent a spring or pond area, where a campsite may also have been located. These animals will constantly keep the topsoil stirred up and aid in the working up of artifacts. I have found many arrowheads on ground literally churned up and half covered with manure. Similarly, I have found many good campsites near old farm and ranch buildings and corrals, such as shown in illustration 115. The reason for this is fairly obvious: The settler generally built farm and ranch houses and livestock facilities near springs or creeks in exactly the same areas that prehistoric people occupied because of the proximity of water or perhaps protection from weather elements. It is easy to overlook the potential of these areas while passing through or obtaining permission to hunt nearby lands. I have actually found stone artifacts right at my feet as I stood visiting with a farmer or rancher in the barnyard while obtaining permission to hunt.

Likewise, an area with a prairie dog colony or excavation by moles or other rodents may be worth examining. These animals will churn up the soil and uncover a surprising number of artifacts. This is especially true if it has recently rained on the freshly dug earth and the area is a good hunting area to begin with. One of my favorite prehistoric campsites on the Colorado-Wyoming border is almost totally covered by two large, separate prairie dog colonies. The prairie dogs

Illustration 137   Typical arrowhead-hunting gear consists of binoculars, hunting stick, camera, canteen, map, and coin purse.

have the same effect as a plow and constantly unearth artifacts at this site. My daughter found three arrowheads in less than forty-five seconds on the surface of dirt excavated by a prairie dog. A word of precaution, however: Be very careful not to reach into a prairie dog hole and take the chance of being bitten by a rattlesnake or an animal that may carry diseases. Furthermore, prairie dog colonies often house many rattlesnakes during the snake season, either in holes or outside of holes. You have to constantly be aware of where you are and where you are walking. Also, in any colony of prairie dogs, you have to be careful where you walk, because the widespread underground tunneling by prairie dogs can cause an area to be susceptible to surface collapse.

My family's favorite camping area is located at a prehistoric campsite. We found many artifacts in the black earth around a spring in areas excavated by moles. The moles seemed to excavate during the night, because each morning upon awakening we could go out and find artifacts in freshly churned black dirt—especially good hunting if it had also rained during the night.

When hunting stone artifacts, travel as lightly as possible. Depending upon weather conditions, you need a hat for protection from the sun, sunscreen, a good jacket with sufficient pockets, a good pair of high-top boots, possibly a pair of gloves, a canteen, a camera, a pocket knife, occasionally a compass, a small first-aid kit including mosquito repellent, a U.S. Geological Survey map of the area, and perhaps a small quantity of food, depending on how long you plan to hunt and how far away from your car you plan to get. Some of these standard hunting accessories are shown in illustration 137. I always try to leave extra pocket space for artifacts and use a small coin purse for arrowheads, since a bag or container is cumbersome to carry. Also, a carpenter's nail apron may be tied around your waist and used easily. It doesn't take very many grinding stones to weigh a person down. Some people like to carry a broom handle with a nail in the end of it or a long-handled dandelion digger for turning flint on the ground without bending over. In recent years I have begun using such a hunting stick, and in an area covered with flint, it definitely saves both time and wear and tear on the lower back. Also, as I have gotten older, I have found that the hunting stick also works well as a cane in rough terrain such as a stream bed or sharp incline.

Such a hunting stick can also be used to turn up a possible grinding stone or to poke around through the sand under a rock overhang. Prehistoric people frequently sought shelter under rock overhangs, where there was protection from the weather. Many nice stone artifacts have been found in sandy areas immediately below or under such overhangs. These areas should only be excavated by the professional archaeologist and any disturbance of the ground should be kept to a minimum—simply poking through the sand rather than digging. Excavation is hard work, disruptive to the natural terrain, and should be left to the professional. I prefer surface hunting only and allow the rodents to do the excavating. All in all, it is really more enjoyable this way.

One final rule of thumb for hunting artifacts: Whenever you find simply a piece of an artifact, always remember to scan the immediate area for several feet and look for the other part that has broken off. If the break in the artifact is clean or straight, there is a good chance it may have happened in recent years, many times by livestock stepping on it. The other piece may be but a few feet away on the surface of the ground. On the other hand, if the break is uneven or shattered, it probably happened upon original impact (in the case of an arrowhead) years or centuries ago, and chances are remote that the remaining part can be found. Even if you cannot find the remaining piece, remember the exact area and prepare a site map. Years later you may be able to go back and find the remaining piece when it has weathered up to the surface.

In hunting artifacts, always look for pictographs and petroglyphs on rock walls and smooth stone surfaces. Petroglyphs are figures incised, scored, or pecked into the surface of the stone, while pictographs are painted figures. Pictographs will ordinarily only be found in caves, rock overhangs, rock shelters, or places protected extremely well from the weather. Petroglyphs, on the other hand, while certainly not invincible to the elements, will withstand weather conditions for many more years. Illustration 138 shows some petroglyphs found in southern Wyoming. While they have withstood the forces of nature, modern humans have managed to disfigure the original designs, which is tragic.

In many areas of the country it is also possible to find potsherds, or pieces of pottery, while hunting stone artifacts. Geographical areas where the climate is not too harsh in the winter months are probably more likely places to find pottery fragments. In most areas of Colorado, for instance, potsherds are difficult to find because most of them have weathered away over the years. Also, some prehistoric cultures simply made more pottery than others. It is far more common to find pieces of pottery in the Southwest, the Midwest, and the eastern United States, for example, than in Colorado (with the exception of southwest Colorado) or Wyoming. There are certain areas of the four-corners region where the ground is literally covered with potsherds. It is possible to find many different styles and types of potsherds depending upon the area in

Illustration 138   Petroglyphs on a rock wall or overhang. Note vandalism by modern humans, which seriously detracts from the ancient art.

which you are hunting. Several of these potsherd types are shown in illustrations 139, 140, and 141. Illustration 140 is actually a potsherd that has been worked into a functional item known as a pot stopper or lid, used to cover the opening of a vaselike jar. Sometimes potsherds are found that have been worked into pendants. Most often these are recognizable not only by the presence of a drilled hole, but also by the shape they have been worked into. In some cases, potsherds are found with a drilled hole that have never been shaped or worked into a pendant. They still look pretty much like a broken piece of pottery. It is my understanding that, on occasion, broken pottery was mended by actually tying broken pieces back together with a twine material—oftentimes yucca fiber. I certainly do not advocate digging for pottery. This is the type of activity that has caused some artifact hunters to be labeled "pot hunter" or "vandal." There is certainly no harm, however, in picking up an occasional piece of pottery while looking for arrowheads and

Illustration 139   Anasazi potsherds found on private land showing different styles of pottery making.

Illustration 140   Anasazi pot stopper fashioned from broken pottery and found on private land.

Illustration 141 Assorted pieces of pottery showing different styles or methods of pottery making. These were found in several Great Plains states.

stone artifacts. Most of these potsherds are out of archaeological context, and in many areas they number into the millions.

There are several good reference books available on pottery, petroglyphs, and pictographs. These subjects are far too broad to be covered in detail in this book, so I have simply discussed their presence and general location. Any study of archaeology, even for the amateur archaeologist, would be incomplete without at least some knowledge of these items.

While hunting artifacts, you may also find many other interesting items from bygone years, both natural and man-made. Some examples are shown in illustrations 142 and 143. I have accumulated old horns of buffalo, deer, and bighorn sheep; together with horseshoes; cow skulls; old gunshot casings, including buffalo gun cartridges; antique barbed wire; nails; and old coins. Some people have even found antique cast-iron toys, marbles, guns, cowboy spurs, and oxen shoes. Also, if you are generally a rock hound as I am, you can find many interest-

Illustration 142   Except for the buffalo horn, this photograph consists almost entirely of assorted modern man-made items that can also be found frequently while hunting stone artifacts.

ing rock and shell specimens, such as those shown in illustration 143. One that comes to mind is the "desert rose," which I have only found in one specific area along the Colorado-Wyoming border. A desert rose is shown at the left end of the center row in illustration 143. There are also literally hundreds of different types of other stones that can be found. Fossils are also frequently found, together with petrified bones and seashells. Meteorites are also occasionally found by arrowhead hunters, although most people, including myself, probably do not recognize them on sight. Anyone with a general interest in nature can also observe wildlife, plant life, and merely enjoy just getting out for a little exercise and fresh air. There are many positive aspects to hunting for arrowheads and stone artifacts besides simply collecting and framing artifacts for display.

Illustration 143 Miscellaneous stone items, including (bottom row, left to right): whetstone, perforated disc, shell fossil, petrified fish or other aquatic animal; (center row, left to right): desert rose, quartz crystal, seashells, fossilized seashell, petrified bone; (top row, left to right): perforated disc, pottery, shell fossil, cup or bowl with round stone ball.

CHAPTER 10

MODERN-DAY FLINTKNAPPING

Anyone who read the first edition of this book would have noticed that I was somewhat critical of modern-day flintknapping. The primary reason for this is that in recent years a great number of contemporary artifacts have been intentionally misrepresented as genuine prehistoric artifacts. This was true fourteen years ago and is unfortunately still true today. Not only are misrepresentations present in a commercial setting, but also in other areas of public display. Reproductions, of course, are not limited to arrowheads and stone artifacts. This phenomenon is true with a vast number of other antiques and historical items. People simply have to educate themselves in order to detect misrepresented items.

Over the years I have gradually changed my mind about modern-day flintknapping; I have tried to educate myself more on the subject, and I have met several modern-day flintknappers. Those whom I have gotten to know are genuinely honest, nice, and sincere and display a high degree of integrity. Not only are they expert flintknappers, they are very knowledgeable about archaeology in general—it really amazes me how much they know. They have gained this knowledge not only by reading published material, but also, in large part, through experience and experimentation in flintknapping.

Professional archaeologists have gained tremendous knowledge about lithic technology in prehistoric times through modern-day flintknapping, and quite a number of professional archaeologists are flintknappers themselves. They have experimented and learned, for example, how the Folsom people fluted a Folsom point—no easy task, to say the least. They have also learned many other techniques of preform or biface reduction, the flaking and notching of projectile points and stone tools. They have learned what it takes to obtain a uniform oblique flaking pattern on the surface of a projectile point as well as the techniques of the delicate pressure-flaking operation and retouch procedures. If you read a book on flintknapping such as those shown in the bibliography of this book, you will discover how technical and scientific flintknapping really is. The application of the principles of physics are present throughout the process of making a projectile point or stone tool. If one understands these principles, the chore of knapping will gradually become easier. Expert flintknappers can produce an average arrowhead in a matter of several minutes, and it is reasonable to conclude that prehistoric man was no different. The archaeological record has shown that these people were very knowledgeable, highly capable, and did, of course, produce the same points and tools as flintknappers do today. They may have, and probably were, more efficient, because their very survival depended upon it. This is the major reason why I have such a tremendous respect for prehistoric peoples and their stone artifacts: They had to improvise, adapt, and construct everything they needed to survive. Professional archaeologists, through flintknapping, have learned a great deal of how they accomplished this.

The principles of flintknapping also involve the study of how stone breaks or fractures with the application of force, either through percussion or pressure flaking. One studying flintknapping will learn, for instance, the difference between an impact fracture caused through the use of the item and a deliberate or perhaps misguided fracture, which occurred during the process of manufacture. Flintknappers have also learned that different types of stone may fracture differently and that some stone material works far easier than others. This type of stone, therefore, was highly sought after, and prehistoric people would transport this material great distances for future use. Many times local stone material in a given area was of poor quality and difficult to work, and imperfections or flaws in the material made flaking extremely difficult. Today, flintknappers have learned and demonstrated all of this, and they have also experimented with heat treating of stone to make knapping easier. Heated stone may take on a different color, and its physical properties may change. Flintknappers in the field will recognize this instantly. They can tell you whether a broken projectile point was broken on impact through use or whether it was broken while being made. Sometimes when a "crude" artifact is found it is obvious to a flintknapper that the person who originally made it gave up and did not finish manufacture because of flaws in the material or general difficulty in working the material. Likewise, a person knowledgeable in flintknapping can usually determine rather quickly when a stone artifact has been reworked or resharpened; there will generally be a slight difference in the flaking pattern between the original flaking and that of the reworked portion. Grinding of edges of a stone artifact in order to assist in hafting is also recognized immediately by an experienced flintknapper. It is obvious to me that a good deal of this knowledge has been gained through experimentation with flintknapping, and for this reason it has a proper place in the study of archaeology.

Flintknapping, above all, is a genuine art form. A beautifully knapped projectile point is truly a work of art and should be respected as such whether made yesterday or ten thousand years ago.

A FURTHER NOTE ON CONTEMPORARY REPRODUCTIONS

Many contemporary reproductions of arrowheads, such as those shown in illustrations 144 and 145, are quite easy to recognize. The flaking of the stone is fresh and sharp to the touch, and it often will

Illustration 144 Three contemporary arrowheads that could be mistaken for genuine prehistoric artifacts.

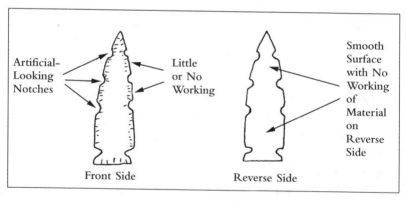

Illustration 145 The contemporary arrowhead, diagrammed.

appear incomplete on the entire surface of the point. Sometimes the other side of the point will hardly show any working at all. Many times these reproductions do in fact appear crude or poorly made; on the other hand, many modern-day flintknappers do an excellent job of flaking and working the stone. Tumbling or sandblasting the material will take away the sharpness of flaking or fresh feel of the object. False patination of stone can now be accomplished in a relatively short period of time as compared with the natural patination process that occurs in nature. Some craftspeople are so adroit in their handling of stone that I sometimes wonder how experts can really determine what is genuine and what is a reproduction—the average person could probably not make this determination. A projectile point made yesterday can literally be made to appear several thousand years old. I have never bought or sold an artifact and never intend to do so, so reproductions will probably not personally affect me. However, I personally do not like the thought of modern-day reproductions being misrepresented as authentic prehistoric artifacts.

CHAPTER 11

DOCUMENTATION AND PRESERVATION

Every collector of stone artifacts should catalog each of the artifacts that he or she finds. Cataloging of artifacts should first involve the exact location where an artifact is found. This can be done directly upon U.S. Geological Survey maps, although in small areas where several artifacts are found, you may have to draw a site map to show the exact locations of discovery. Cataloging and mapping may seem unnecessary at first when your overall number of artifacts is small, but as time goes by and the number of artifacts increases, it is next to impossible to remember exactly where you have found each one. As a general scientific proposition, much can also be learned from relative location of artifacts in the field.

In cataloging and mapping, it is mandatory that each artifact be numbered and listed in a journal or log book. I have always used a very fine-pointed black-ink pen to write the assigned number on the surface of the artifact. It is usually a good idea to clean the surface first with soap and water so that the ink will adhere better. It has also been my experience that, over time, black ink will fade away, perhaps due mainly to sunlight if the artifact is kept or displayed in natural light. I have found that if I allow the ink to fully dry, I can then place a small amount of clear fingernail polish over the number, and this will generally prevent it from fading or disappearing altogether. I learned the hard way in numbering our collection, for at one point in time, I had to completely renumber all of our artifacts because I had failed to use clear fingernail polish. These artifacts now appear to be holding up quite well, and the numbers are no longer disappearing like they once did. I have seen other colors of ink used, but white ink, for example, seems to more adversely affect the appearance of most artifacts. (This would obviously depend upon the color of the artifact itself.) Black ink is usually far less conspicuous and yet fully visible upon close inspection. White ink is also not nearly as available as black ink and may be more expensive. On a black artifact you may have to use white ink or prepare the surface with white correction fluid before using black ink. It is my understanding that invisible ink is now available, but it has to be viewed under a special light and would, no doubt, be more expensive.

There are probably several methods of numbering that a person could use. I am most familiar with two of these methods: First, artifacts can simply be numbered from one on up ad infinitum. This method may work fine to begin with, but as the numbers get higher, it can be quite frustrating placing the number 1,020 on a very small birdpoint. Second, a combination of numbering and lettering may also work well. In this method, each site is given a number, or a letter that is then followed by a number. A corresponding journal would detail various sites by number or letter and then be followed by the number of the specific artifact. On larger sites where a significiant number of artifacts are found, this method, too, could result in large numbers that need to be written on small artifacts. Perhaps one way to minimize this problem would be to restrict this lettering and numbering procedure to individual counties within a given geographical area. One thing is clear, however, and that is that cataloging is really not that difficult and can be accomplished without insurmountable problems. It is quite subjective and simply may come down to a matter of individual preference.

Aside from location, artifacts should be cataloged as to the date found, color and type of flint material or other material used for the artifact, and the type of artifact itself; e.g., arrowhead, knife, scraper, etc. This information should all be written in the journal and kept in a safe location. Some collectors also prefer to photograph each individual artifact, and while this is nice to do, it can be quite expensive. Some people have simply chosen to keep photographic records of unusually nice, complete artifacts rather than every item. Another recommended procedure is to photograph individual sites. This creates a permanent record and complements a journal quite nicely. Many times collectors also like to photograph artifacts in situ prior to removing the artifact from its location. This, too, is an informative addition to the cataloging operation.

Cataloging and mapping, together with site photography, are very important prerequisites to scientific archaeology and have always divided the amateur from the professional. Perhaps if the amateur archaeologist or collector were more careful with this aspect of collecting, he or she would command more respect from the professional and even escape the labels of "looter" or "vandal."

In the preservation of stone artifacts, one decision that has to be made is whether the artifact should be cleaned and/or polished. As mentioned previously, one may have to clean the surface of an artifact prior to marking it during the cataloging process. It would be difficult to mark a dirty artifact just as it came from the field. I prefer to wash my artifacts with a solution of warm water and dishwashing soap. An old toothbrush does a good job to help remove soil and mineral stains and bring out the natural beauty of the flint material, ordinarily successfully getting into and cleaning the small cracks and crevices created during the original flaking of the material. Obviously, using any kind of a steel brush could damage the artifact. I have met a few collectors who have polished stone artifacts with various polishing products, but I have never done this because it seems to create an unnatural appearance. Furthermore, many artifacts found in riverbeds could already be polished by running water or through the action of sand after a period of many years. If other artifacts are polished, it might create a false impression that these artifacts have been polished naturally. It is also nice to maintain such a distinction when comparing different artifacts in a collection.

The natural process known as patination is a condition whereby minerals in the soil actually accumulate on the surface of another stone material after many hundreds or thousands of years. In some cases, this patina literally permeates the stone material and, in essence, becomes a part of the material itself. This is very difficult, if not impossible, to remove with a toothbrush and soapy water. You would almost have to use an acid solution or scrape off the patina with a steel knife or blade. When attempting this, it is easy to permanently damage the surface of the artifact, and it could also be dangerous. For this reason, I never attempt to remove patina. Furthermore, the archaeological value of the artifact may be lost by removing patina, since it usually indicates a more ancient artifact. The patina may also indicate something about the original archaeological context of the artifact. Patination can, and often does, entirely change the visual appearance of an artifact. Even though it may be tempting to remove the patina in order to reveal the colorful flint material, I do not recommend doing so.

Over the years, many outstanding artifact collections have wound up hidden in attic trunks, basement boxes, and coffee cans—often in the possession of someone who could care less what they are, where they came from, and where they are going to end up. In my opinion, this is tragic—artifacts perhaps thousands of years old simply being ignored, neglected, and forgotten. Eventually these collections of artifacts end up sold at auction, and entire collections are divided up and sold to different individuals. Sometimes catalogs are lost or destroyed and no longer accompany the collection—if, indeed, there ever was one. Occasionally, people inherit artifact collections that are likewise neglected or dispersed in a similar fashion.

If no one is interested in an artifact collection that has been found or inherited, it should at least be donated to a local museum. Many artifacts have, of course, been donated, but all too often this is not the case. Incidentally, there are hundreds of small, local, often rural museums throughout the country that house many of the more outstanding collections of stone artifacts and have them on public display. Many larger, well-known museums have plenty of stone artifacts in storage but oftentimes have none displayed publicly. In my opinion, an artifact worth keeping and preserving is an artifact worth displaying.

There are many ways you can display artifacts. Picture-frame or shadowbox designs for wall mounting are probably the most common. With this method, there is practically no limit to the number of designs that can be used. Even broken arrowheads and other artifacts can be arranged in attractive, eye-catching designs. (See illustration 146 for a good example of how to do this.) I typically find at least ten broken artifacts for each whole artifact, so there are always plenty to display. Perfect arrowheads, of course, are very attractive displayed in frames, as are knives, scrapers, drills, and awls. (A framed display of perfect arrowheads is shown in illustration 147.) Years ago, I made several frames from old, gray, weathered lumber. I still prefer these over frames and shadowboxes purchased in stores. These frames, however, can be quite difficult to put glass in, and unless a person is quite capable with this type of work, he or she may be better off purchasing glassed-in shadowboxes. Unfortunately, shadowboxes with glass are about the only safe way to publicly display stone artifacts.

Larger, heavier artifacts such as grinding stones, grinding slabs, grooved hammers, and axes are ordinarily not suitable for framing and wall display unless a person is quite capable of this type of work. These artifacts can be displayed nicely without much trouble in open or enclosed shelves or table-top shadowboxes that are protected by glass or other transparent material.

Protection of stone artifacts is the primary concern when any public display is considered. Obviously, loose artifacts will disappear more quickly than those that are better secured and protected. I have always used Elmer's glue when attaching stone artifacts in frames; generally only a small amount is required. This glue is strong enough to hold the average artifact in place and yet enable it to be detached without much trouble if need be. A fast-bonding glue will be much harder, if not impossible, to remove an artifact from in case a rearrangement is desired.

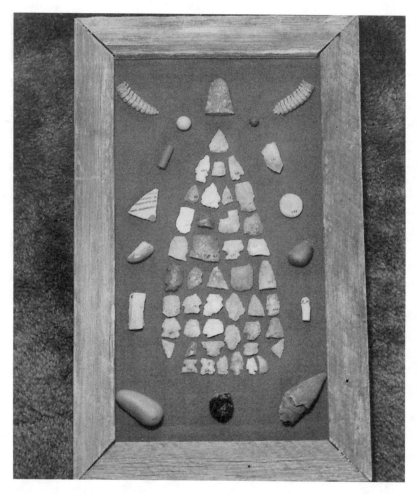

Illustration 146   An arrowhead design frame that also contains interesting miscellaneous finds.

Some people use Velcro to attach artifacts in frames, and some will glue artifacts to the head of a raised pin. This last method creates a unique appearance in the frame. If you are more creative, you could probably come up with many other interesting methods of attaching and displaying stone artifacts. Experiment and choose the method that you prefer.

Illustration 147   An arrowhead frame that contains some of the better arrowheads in the author's family collection.

Two newer methods of stone-artifact preservation involve artifact restoration and what I refer to as plastic casts. I am really not very familiar with the particulars and details of artifact restoration and plastic casts—in some instances individuals have their own techniques, which are probably unknown to most people.

Artifact restoration generally involves replacing the broken or missing portion of an artifact with a plasticlike, synthetic material. Most arrowhead hunters have found many beautiful artifacts that are only missing a tip, one edge, or a portion of a base. Obviously, if these missing portions are artificially replaced by an expert craftsperson, the artifact becomes even more attractive. An excellent craftsperson can actually create a finished product that cannot be visually distinguished from an original, whole piece—the only way to do so is to feel the surface. If these restored artifacts are labeled as such and no deception is involved, I can see nothing wrong in such activity.

Illustration 148   Assorted artifact frames in the author's family collection.

Plastic casting involves using a mold to duplicate an entire artifact with a plasticlike, synthetic material. A talented craftsperson can actually duplicate an entire stone artifact so effectively that the only way a person can tell the difference is by touch or feel. The plastic-cast artifact will be noticeably lighter in weight and will feel like plastic, but it will look exactly like the original stone artifact. Sometimes, if a person donates an artifact to a museum or university, it will provide that person with a plastic cast of the artifact to retain. It is certainly a nice way to donate an artifact for scientific purposes and yet still "keep" the artifact at the same time. Many times I have been with individuals who have found beautiful artifacts—ones that I wish I could have found. Plastic casts are an excellent way to "have" such artifacts in your own collection. I have a nice group of plastic casts of well-known Paleo points. These are attractively displayed in my home, and I have enjoyed them. Plastic casting is certainly a good way to preserve an artifact so that more than one person can enjoy it.

CHAPTER 12

ORGANIZATIONS AND ACTIVITIES

Most amateur archaeologists are very anxious to learn more about archaeology. Many of the available publications on the subject are very scientific in nature and for many people are very difficult to understand. It has always surprised me how technical archaeology really is.

Over the years I have learned very much about archaeology by simply visiting with people who are interested in and knowledgeable about the field. I suppose that in some cases the information I obtained was not reliable nor correct, but I think in the vast majority of instances I did receive valid information. In several cases, later reading of archaeological material proved that what I had heard earlier really was true.

In order for people to get together and discuss archaeology, one must have the opportunity to do so. One of the best things an arrowhead hunter can do is join a local archaeological society or association. There are a vast number of these organizations throughout the United States—far more than most people would realize. Most states, for example, have a state archaeological society that hosts many educational activities throughout the year. Normally, these societies have local chapters, and there could easily be one in your area. Before you join one of these societies, however, you should find out what their policies and requirements are. Many of these organizations, for instance, do not believe in, or advocate, private collecting of stone artifacts. Naturally, an arrowhead hunter with a private collection would want to know about this beforehand in order to avoid an awkward situation. Perhaps, in some cases, an artifact collector could simply attend lectures and presentations as a periodic guest without actually joining this type of association. As stated earlier, one can learn much about archaeology by simply listening to others or attending lectures.

A very interesting program called the Program for Avocational Archaeological Certification, otherwise known as the PAAC Survey Program, has been conducted through the Denver office of the Colorado State Archaeologist. This program consists of a series of courses on anthropology and archaeology and related scientific aspects, including dating methods. Site survey and laboratory analysis are also covered in the program, together with fieldwork procedures. This program has been very worthwhile and educational, and it may go a long way toward bringing amateur and professional archaeologists into closer harmony and cooperation.

Aside from the various state archaeological societies, there are many private and/or local associations and societies that exist throughout the country. These organizations are geared more toward the individual who hunts and collects stone artifacts, and, obviously, there are not strict limitations nor requirements regarding these activities. In most cases, these organizations also provide worthwhile and educational activities on a regular basis. One such organization to which I belong is The Loveland Archaeological Society, Inc., a Colorado nonprofit corporation, in Loveland, Colorado. This organization and its predecessors have existed in one form or another for the past sixty years. There are regular monthly meetings with archaeological or historical programs, and field trips are conducted regularly during the summer. The society also has an extensive library of archaeological materials, and some organizations even publish informative quarterly journals (see the recommended reading list at the conclusion of this book). Members frequently get together to compare and exchange ideas and knowledge, often at meetings and on field trips. This organization is comprised of a number of people, almost all amateurs, who are very knowledgeable about archaeology. Many have gained tremendous respect from the professional community and, in some cases, actually work together with professional archaeologists on various projects. Aside from reading, this is how I have increased my knowledge of archaeology over the years. Again, there are many more of these organizations than most people would think—you just have to seek them out. Sometimes you can do this through word of mouth, written materials, or perhaps in some cases through a chamber of commerce.

One national organization that came into existence a few years ago is the American Society for Amateur Archaeology, headquartered in Buffalo, New York. This organization is headed by Dr. R. Michael Gramly, a professional archaeologist. The organization publishes an informative biannual journal (see the recommended reading list at the end of this book), each issue focusing on a particular state of the United States and providing a nice rundown of significant sites. Regular, professionally conducted fieldwork projects are held throughout the United States, and members are welcome to participate. Dr. Gramly recognizes the noteworthy contributions of amateurs to the study of archaeology, and he organized this society in order to further their participation and to aid in preserving the rights of individuals who collect archaeological artifacts.

As a collection grows and gains in prominence and respectability, the day may come when public display might be appropriate. A museum, of course, is the most obvious place for public display and future preservation. However, many museums nowadays will simply store stone artifacts in a basement or storage area, not available for viewing by the general public. In fact, many times the artifacts are totally unavailable to anyone who wants to look at them. Many fine collections have not been given to museums for exactly this reason. Other than

Illustration 149   Loveland Archaeological Society field trip.

museums and occasional store-window display, artifact shows are probably the only other chance for public display. Many of these shows, however, are trade shows where commercial activity takes place and, as such, may be frowned upon by professionals, government authorities, and others. It is my understanding that there are many of these shows held on a regular basis, particularly throughout the central United States. These events can be very educational and worthwhile, and they are extremely popular.

One annual event, however, that stands out among all the rest, and that is highly educational and strictly noncommercial, is the Loveland Stone Age Fair. This show is held annually in Loveland, Colorado, on the last full weekend in September, and it is sponsored jointly by the city of Loveland and the Loveland Archaeological Society, Inc. A vast number of stone artifacts are displayed almost entirely by amateur archaeologists from throughout the United States. Collectors have participated in this event for more than sixty years—first in Cornish, Colorado, where the event started in 1934, and then,

Illustration 150   Allen Crawford of the Loveland Archaeological Society, shown with the Stone Age Fair history exhibit at the Loveland Museum and Gallery of Loveland, Colorado. Allen has been instrumental in the author's development as an amateur archaeologist over the years.

since 1940, in Loveland, Colorado, at the Pulliam Community Building. Programs feature professional and amateur speakers each year. The list of speakers who have appeared over the years is a virtual "who's who" among prominent professional archaeologists from throughout the country. Most professionals appreciate the integrity of this educational event and respect the sincere efforts of those who

Illustration 151   1994 Loveland Stone Age Fair speakers, shown left to right: C. G. Yeager, Garry Weinmeister, and Dr. Richard Michael Gramly of Buffalo, New York, one of the primary investigators of the Wenatchee, Washington, Clovis site and organizer of the American Society of Amateur Archaeology.

host it. This coming together of both amateurs and professionals and the resulting exchange of ideas and analysis of data is a very worthwhile endeavor. It brings the amateur and professional interests together in a spirit of cooperation and results in valuable knowledge that can be passed on to future generations for further archaeological study.

Illustration 152 The author at the Folsom Museum in Folsom, New Mexico, a short distance from the original Folsom discovery by George McJunkin, a black cowboy.

GLOSSARY

GENERAL DEFINITIONS OF COMMONLY USED ARCHAEOLOGICAL TERMS

abrader. Any stone material with abrasive qualities showing evidence (usually a groove or flattened surface) of polishing, grinding, or smoothing operations.

adze. A stone tool usually constructed out of flint material and used most often in woodworking, similarly to a chisel.

all-purpose tool. A stone tool that is usually made of flint material and normally found with a point and a worked edge, which could be used as a drill, graver, scraper, or knife without further modification.

amulet. An ornamental or ceremonial object usually made of stone, bone, shell, or perhaps broken pottery that is sometimes found with perforated holes.

anvil. A smoothed and often grooved handheld stone that is most often used in the paddle-and-anvil method of pottery making.

Apache tear. Small and irregular-shaped obsidian stones that may have been used ceremonially.

archaeology. The study of historic or prehistoric peoples and their cultures by analysis of the artifacts they have left behind.

Archaic. Generally, the archaeological time period of 6,000 B.C. to 1,000 B.C.

arrow. The wooden shaft used with the arrowhead or projectile point, which had feathers on the opposite end to aid the arrow in flight.

arrowhead. The stone, or sometimes bone, point used as the puncturing device on the end of an arrow opposite the end with the feathers.

artifact. Any object that has been made or modified by human beings of previous cultures.

atlatl. A device used to throw a spear in order to obtain greater distance, stability, and speed than a hand-thrown spear.

atlatl weight. A stone that was usually smoothed, grooved, and sometimes perforated, used with the atlatl and as additional weight and for balance.

awl. Pointed tool made from stone or bone used for perforation of other items such as skins, hides, or wood; also used in basketmaking and weaving.

awl pointer. A handheld abrasive stone used to sharpen or repoint awls; contains a thinner groove than that found on an abrader.

axe. A handheld or grooved and hafted stone shaped by chipping, pecking, or abrading, which is sometimes polished, and is used for cutting or chopping purposes.

axe sharpener. An abrasive stone used for sharpening axe blades with grooved or depressed signs of wear or use.

balls (stone). Round stone balls were either naturally round or formed by pecking and were probably used in games.

bannerstone. Generally, a stone artifact formed by pecking, grinding, and polishing, usually barrel-shaped or winged in appearance, used for ceremonial and ornamental purposes or perhaps as atlatl weights.

beads. Small ornamental objects made not only of shell, clay, bone, but also of stone. They were usually perforated and strung as necklaces and bracelets.

bifacial. The condition of flint material after having been worked on both sides.

birdpoint. A small projectile point often assumed to be used for hunting birds or small animals but also quite capable for hunting large animals.

blade. A thin piece of flint material, generally worked on both sides, used as a knife for cutting purposes.

blank. A rough-shaped item, usually made of stone or pottery, that is intended for later refinement into a finished point, tool, or other artifact. Similar to, or the same as, a preform.

blow-out. A wind-blown, hollowed-out depression in the ground that normally consists of light or sandy soil.

buffalo jump. A steep incline, such as a ridge or a cliff, where buffalo were crowded off the edge to a landing area below for slaughtering or butchering.

buffalo wallow. Usually a depressed area of the landscape that contains water, where buffalo gathered.

burin. A stone tool made from flint material with one end finely worked and used for cutting or incising such as a chisel or graver.

camprock. The assemblage of flint material, hard stones, and river rocks that are found out of place with the natural surroundings, which indicates the presence of an ancient campsite.

celt. A stone axe that is either handheld or grooved for hafting, often used interchangably with the term *axe*. Some axes or celts were also used for ceremonial purposes.

chips. Small flakes of the flint materials that result from the flintknapping process used in making stone objects. They are sometimes used as tools, such as knives and gravers, without modification.

chisel. A tool, sometimes made of stone, with sharpened ends, that was used for shaping or splitting wood.

chopper. A stone tool with a rough, chipped edge used for chopping or pounding other materials.

conchoidal fracture. The characteristic manner in which flint material breaks apart upon percussion or pressure flaking.

concretion. Natural stones composed of different rocks or minerals formed together, which might look like body parts or animal excrement, used as charms or ceremonially.

cooking stones. Round stone balls, either formed naturally or by pecking, that were primarily used to heat water used in cooking.

core. A residual piece of flint material that remains after the removal of flakes during the flintknapping process. It is usually somewhat larger and thicker than the flakes that were removed.

crescent. A curved knife with a finely worked edge.

crystals. Hexagonal or irregular pieces of quartz, often clear or white in color, that were sometimes altered and used ornamentally or ceremonially.

debitage. The assortment or collection of flint material or other camprock found at an archaeological site and resulting from human activity.

desert varnish. A form of patination that results in the change of coloration of flint material over a substantial period of time.

disc. Pieces of thin, round stone or pottery that sometimes contained one or more perforated holes and were used ornamentally, ceremonially, or in games. Some discs were also used as spindle whorls in weaving operations.

drill. Narrow, pointed stone tools, delicately chipped and often T-shaped, that were generally hafted and used for perforation of other objects. Many drills are broken arrowheads that have been reworked with the notches left in place and used in hafting.

effigy. Generally, a man-made likeness of human or animal objects made from flint material or hard stone material, bone, shell, or pottery.

erosion. The natural process of deterioration or dimishment of the soil or geological features. This can be caused by weathering or, in some cases, human or animal activity.

fetish. Generally, animal figurines made of stone or potsherds that were used primarily for ceremonial purposes.

flaker. Generally, an antler tine used in the flaking process by a flintknapper.

flakes. Pieces of flint material removed from a core during the flintknapping process that were used to make projectile points and stone tools. Also referred to as *chips* or *spalls.*

flesher. Generally, a handheld stone or bone tool with a sharp edge used to remove fat, hair, or flesh from hides.

flintknapping. The process in which humans work or modify flint material to make tools, projectile points, and other objects by chipping, flaking, or working the stone.

flint material. A general reference to stone material used by ancient people, including, but not limited to, quartzite, quartz, felsite, basalt, agate, chalcedony, petrified wood, obsidian, jasper, and chert.

foreign material. Generally, flint material or hard stone that is present in an area where it would not normally be found.

foreshaft. A short, cylindrical piece of wood that contains a hafted arrowhead or spearpoint and that was inserted into the end of an arrowshaft or spearshaft.

gaming piece. A stone, pottery, or bone piece that is usually shaped or smoothed to a flat surface and is sometimes found with marks incised thereon, commonly used as a counter in gaming activities.

gem point. A projectile point made from agate, chalcedony, or other type of gemstones.

geofact. A chipped or altered piece of flint material resulting from natural forces rather than human activity that is not an artifact at all.

gorget. A stone or pottery piece with one or more perforated holes that was used as an ornament or ceremonial object.

graver. A small scraperlike tool that contains one or more delicately worked points used for scoring or incising other objects or materials.

grinding slab. A flat stone, such as a metate, used to grind other materials.

grinding stone. Ordinarily a fist-size stone with abrasive qualities (oftentimes a river-worn rock) used most often with a metate or grinding slab to grind other materials.

hafting. The process in which a stone tool or projectile point is attached to a handle or shaft.

hammerstone. A fist-size stone similar to a grinding stone but used to hammer or pound other material rather than grind. Will usually contain evidence of pecking or chipping rather than rubbing or grinding.

hearth. A fire-blackened portion of the earth, which often indicates the presence of prehistoric activity.

heavy soil. Generally, soil composed of clay or shale that does not weather or deteriorate quickly or significantly.

hoe. A chipped and shaped larger piece of stone, either handheld or grooved for hafting, that is used like a modern garden hoe.

hunting stick. A stick or shaft used to move stones on the ground by someone who is surface hunting artifacts.

incised. The physical condition of an artifact that has had lines or marks scored upon its surface through the use of another tool.

in situ. Used to describe the location of an artifact as found in its original context upon or in the ground.

kill site. The geographical location where game animals were killed and butchered by prehistoric people for later use as food, clothing, or shelter.

knife. A thin, carefully flaked tool most often made from one of the flint materials. It was either handheld or hafted to a bone, antler, or wood handle and used as any knife would be used today.

light soil. Generally, soil composed of sand or fine loam that weathers or deteriorates quickly and significantly.

macroblade. A large stone blade or knife with at least one finely worked edge used for cutting purposes.

mano. A fist-size piece of stone with abrasive qualities (oftentimes a river-worn rock and sometimes deliberately shaped) that was handheld and used with the metate to grind materials. It is very similar to the grinding stone and is always flattened on one or more sides or ends.

maul. A stone artifact similar to a hammerstone that was always grooved for hafting. Similar to the modern-day hammer.

metate. A large, flat stone with a smooth surface made by grinding or rubbing with a mano or grinding stone. Many variations are found, some with sides or a trough and a deeply worn surface, some with a hole worn through the entire stone. A boulder metate is a worn or indented surface on a large stone boulder or surface.

microblade. A small stone blade or knife with at least one finely worked edge that was used for cutting purposes.

mortar. A hard stone material, such as granite, that has been shaped and indented by pecking and that serves as a bowl for use with the pestle. Boulder mortars also exist, which are similar to boulder metates.

native material. Generally, flint material or hard stone in an area where it is found naturally.

native soil. Generally, the condition of soil or ground that has never been altered by humans.

needle. Normally made from bone or shell and used in sewing operations as a needle would be used today. It often had a perforated hole on one end.

notches. Indentations worked into flint material or hard stone so it could be hafted to a shaft or handle.

outcropping. The natural presence of flint material or other stone on the surface of the ground.

overhang. Generally, a large rock or assortment of rocks found naturally in position, resulting in a partially covered area of the ground used for shelter. Also referred to as a *rock shelter.*

paint cup. Generally, a hollowed-out small stone, like sandstone, formed by pecking and used to mix paint materials. Similar to a small mortar.

Paleo. Generally, the archaeological time period of 20,000 B.C. to 6,000 B.C.

patination. The process of chemical change to a substance that occurs over a period of years and results in a change of appearance through the buildup of chemicals or mellowing of coloration. *See also* desert varnish.

pecking. The physical process of chipping one hard stone material by another hard stone material.

pendant. A perforated object made of stone, bone, pottery, or shell that was used for ornamental purposes, such as a necklace. Many were shaped, abraded, and smoothed and were quite colorful.

pendant blank. An unperforated piece of stone, bone, shell, or pottery intended for future use as a pendant.

percussion. A flintknapping term used to describe the process of flaking a flint material, either directly by striking it with another stone or indirectly through the use of another object, such as an intermediary striking surface.

pestle. A stone tool shaped for pounding or grinding that is generally cylindrical in appearance and used with a mortar.

petroglyph. A prehistoric artwork that is pecked, chipped, or incised upon larger stone surfaces through the use of hammerstones, choppers, or any hard stone tool.

pictograph. A prehistoric artwork that is painted upon larger stone surfaces and is generally found in caves, rock shelters, or other locations protected from the weather.

pipe. Generally, a stone, clay, or wood object that has been shaped and sometimes decorated and is intended for smoking purposes that are ordinarily ceremonial in nature.

plastering stone. A hard stone tool, generally made of granite, basalt, or sometimes sandstone, that is similar to a mano or grinding stone but normally has a finger groove on each side to aid in use during masonry operations. Some plastering stones have been found with masonry material adhered to them, sometimes with fingerprints still visible.

plummet. Generally, a hard stone that has been shaped similarly to a plumb bob, containing one groove. Used for ceremonial or ornamental purposes or perhaps as a sinker for fishing.

polish. The smoothed or shiny appearance of an artifact that results from the process of making or using the item.

pot stopper. A round-shaped piece of stone or pottery used as a cover or lid for pots or other vessels.

potsherd. A broken piece of pottery.

preform. A worked or chipped piece of flint material that has been roughly shaped to resemble the tool or point that will result after further refinement, chipping, or flaking at a future time. Also referred to as a *blank*.

pressure flaking. The process during flintknapping whereby delicate flaking is performed on flint material, often through the use of an antler, which results in a sharp point or finely worked edge.

projectile point. An arrowhead or spearpoint.

quarry. Generally, a natural outcropping of flint material or stone where prehistoric people mined stone for use in making tools, projectile points, and other items.

quarry blank. A roughed-out piece of flint material (*see* preform) that was often worked at the site of a stone quarry and later refined to a finished item.

reamer. A hand drill normally made from flint material that was used to ream out or enlarge holes in other substances. This was sometimes fashioned from broken arrowheads and often referred to simply as a *drill*.

reworked point or tool. A projectile point or stone tool resharpened or worked from a larger point or tool that had been broken or dulled from usage.

Many stone knives were repeatedly resharpened after heavy usage and are today very much smaller than originally made.

river rock. A water-worn or smoothed hard stone found in a river or creek bed and used as a tool, ornamental, or ceremonial item.

rubbing stone. Generally, a hard stone implement, often a river rock, that has been smoothed or polished from handheld use in working hides, pottery, or other substances.

saw. A cutting tool made from stone or bone that contains teeth or a deeply serrated edge as opposed to a finely pressure-flaked edge of a stone knife.

scraper. A shaped stone tool made of any flint material with a finely chipped working edge used for scraping or cutting purposes. These often have working on one side only, with the underside being smooth or concave. Also referred to as *thumb scrapers, side scrapers, end scrapers,* and *spokeshaves,* depending on the location of the working edge. Some scrapers were also notched for hafting purposes.

serrated edge. A finely worked, sawtoothlike edge that is pressure flaked on a tool or projectile point to be more efficient for cutting or penetrating.

shaft. The wooden handle of a hafted tool or the wooden spear used with a projectile point.

shaft straightener. Generally, a shaped, hard stone tool, also called an *abrader,* that contains one or more grooves and is used in the hand to scrape or polish a shaft rather than to straighten it, although some straightening could possibly result.

sinew. A finely cut strip of leather, hide, muscle, or tendon used in the hafting process or in sewing operations.

sinker. Generally, hard stone weights, often water-worn stones, that were grooved or perforated for use in fishing. Some light, porous stone materials were grooved or perforated for use as floats or bobbers.

site. The geographical location of a campsite, lookout site, quarry site, hunting site, or kill site where prehistoric activity occurred.

slitter. A stone knife made of flint material and notched for hafting to a shaft that was used to slit or cut other materials.

soil heaving. The physical act of soil rising as an effect of the freezing and thawing of the ground.

spall. A piece or flake of flint material that has been struck from a core during the flintknapping process.

spatulate. A hard stone or flint tool used as a chisel or knife to work hides or wood.

spear. A throwing or thrusting shaft made of wood to use with the spearpoint, which was generally mounted on the end of a foreshaft and inserted into the end of the spear.

spearpoint. Normally, a large projectile point made most often from one of the flint materials to use with the spear. Some Paleo spearpoints, however, were unusually small. Many stone knives notched or stemmed for hafting are mistakenly referred to as spearpoints.

spokeshave. Generally, a scraper or any piece of flint material with an edge that could be used to scrape other materials, such as a wood shaft or arrow. Some spokeshaves have one or more notches on the edges.

stray find. An artifact that is found alone on the surface of an area not associated with any particular prehistoric site that would normally contain debitage or other artifacts.

Tang knife. A stone knife made of flint material that is notched on one corner for hafting to a shaft or handle.

tepee ring. A ring or circle of larger stones found on the surface of the ground that indicates the former presence of a tepee or ceremonial location.

unifacial. The condition of flint material after it has been worked only on one side.

unworked material. A piece of hard stone or flint material that has not been modified by humans.

utilized flake. Any piece of flint material that could be used as a tool without further modification or flintknapping work. *See also* knife, graver, and scraper.

volcanic material. Generally, stone material, such as basalt, pumice, obsidian, and Apache tears, that results from the activity of volcanos.

weathered. The physical change in appearance or structure of an item or the ground as a result of the natural activity of weather conditions, usually over an extended period of time.

wedge. A good-size piece of flint material that has been worked and shaped in order to break apart other materials through use, just like a modern-day wedge.

whetstone. Usually a flattened piece of sandstone or hard stone material that was pecked or shaped for handheld use to sharpen tools, such as axes, or other implements with a sharpened edge.

Woodland. Generally, the archaeological time period of 1,000 B.C. to A.D. 1,500.

worked material. Hard stone or flint material that has been altered or modified by human activity, such as flintknapping.

RECOMMENDED READING

The Amateur Archaeologist (biannual). Journal of the American Society for Amateur Archaeology, P.O. Box 1264, Buffalo, NY 14205.

Central States Archaeological Journal (quarterly). John H. Beyes, Business Manager, 11552 Patty Ann Drive, St. Louis, MO 63146-5471.

Chips (quarterly). Flint Knappers' Guild International, P.O. Box 702, Branson, MO 65616.

Discovering Archaeology (bimonthly). 1205 N. Oregon Street, El Paso, TX 79902.

Indian Artifact Magazine (quarterly). 245 Fairview Road, Turbotville, PA 17772-9599.

Mammoth Trumpet (quarterly). Center for the Study of the First Americans, Oregon State University, 355 Weniger Hall, Corvallis, OR 97331-6510.

Ohio Archaeologist (quarterly). The Archaeological Society of Ohio, 138 Ann Court, Lancaster, OH 43130-3416.

Plains Anthropologist (quarterly). Plains Anthropological Society, 410 Wedgewood Drive, Lincoln, NE 68510.

Texas Cache Magazine (quarterly). Texas Amateur Archaeological Association, 8901 S. Highway 67, No. 10, San Angelo, TX 76904.

BIBLIOGRAPHY

Barnett, Franklin. *Dictionary of Prehistoric Indian Artifacts of the American Southwest* (1973. Reprint, Flagstaff, Ariz.: Northland Publishing Company, 1991).

Bell, Robert E. *Guide to the Identification of Certain American Indian Projectile Points.* Special Bulletin No. 1. Oklahoma Anthropological Society, December 1958.

————. *Guide to the Identification of Certain American Indian Projectile Points.* Special Bulletin No. 2. Oklahoma Anthropological Society, October 1960.

Benson, Laurel. *Colorado from Indians to Industry* (Loveland, Colo.: Center for In-Service Education, Inc., 1975).

Bradford, George. *Paleo Points.* Vol. 1. Ont., Canada: George R. Bradford, 1976.

Brennan, Louis A. *Beginner's Guide to Archaeology* (Harrisburg, Pa.: The Stackpole Company, 1973).

Celoria, Francis. *Archaeology* (New York: Bantam, 1973).

Chesterman, Charles W. *National Audubon Society Field Guide to North American Rocks and Minerals* (New York: Alfred A. Knopf, Inc., 1979).

Coenraads, Robert R; Paul Willis; and David Roots. *Rocks & Fossils.* Edited by Arthur B. Busbey III. Sydney, San Francisco, London: Weldon Owen Pty Limited, Time-Life Books, U.S. Weldon Owen, Inc., 1996.

Colorado Revised Statutes (1999). Section 24-80-401 through 24-80-411. C.R.S. 1963 (Historical, Prehistorical and Archaeological Resources).

Colorado Revised Statutes (1999). Section 24-80-1301 through 24-80-1305. C.R.S. 1990, Senate Bill 90 (Unmarked Human Graves).

Frison, George C. *Prehistoric Hunters of the High Plains* (New York: Academic Press, Inc., 1978).

————. *Prehistoric Hunters of the High Plains.* 2d ed. (San Diego, Calif.: Academic Press, Inc., 1991).

Frison, George C., and Dennis J. Stanford. *The Agate Basin Site* (New York: Academic Press, Inc., 1982).

Haynes, Vance, and George Agogino. *Geological Significance of a New Radiocarbon Date from the Lindenmeier Site* (Denver, Colo.: The Denver Museum of Natural History, 1960).

Hibben, Frank C. *Digging Up America* (New York: Hill and Wang, 1960).

————. *The Lost Americans* (New York: Thomas Y. Crowell Company, 1946, 1968).

Hothem, Lar. *North American Indian Artifacts* (Florence, Ala.: Books Americana, Inc., 1978).

Hughes, J. Donald. *American Indians in Colorado* (Boulder, Colo.:Pruett Publishing Company, 1977).

Irwin, H. J., and C. C. Irwin. *Excavations at the Lo Dais Ka Site in the Denver, Colorado, Area* (Denver, Colo.: The Denver Museum of Natural History, 1959).

Irwin-Williams, Cynthia, and Henry J. Irwin. *Excavations at Magic Mountain* (Denver, Colo.: The Denver Museum of Natural History, 1966).

Knudson, Ruthann, and Bennie C. Keel, eds. *The Public Trust and the First Americans* (Corvallis, Oreg.: Oregon State University Press for the Center for the Study of the First Americans, 1995).

Look, Al. *1,000 Million Years on the Colorado Plateau, Land of Uranium* (Denver, Colo.: Bell Publications, 1955).

Meltzer, David J. *Search for the First Americans* (Montreal, Canada: St. Remy Press, 1993).

Moore, Earl F. *Silent Arrows, Indian Lore and Artifact Hunting* (Klamath Falls, Oreg.: Paul Tremaine Publishing, 1977).

Murray, Robert A. *Pipes on the Plains* (Minn.: The Pipestone Indian Shrine Association and National Park Service, United States Department of Interior, 1968, 1975).

———. *Pipestone, A History* (Minn.: The Pipestone Indian Shrine Association and National Park Service, United States Department of Interior, 1965).

Oppelt, Norman T. *Earth, Water and Fire—The Prehistoric Pottery of Mesa Verde* (Greeley, Colo.: Oppelt Publications, 1991, 1998).

Patten, Bob. *Old Tools—New Eyes: A Primal Primer of Flintknapping* (Lakewood, Colo.: Stone Dagger Publications, 1999).

Perino, Gregory. *Guide to the Identification of Certain American Indian Projectile Points.* Special Bulletin No. 3. Oklahoma Anthropological Society, October 1968.

———. *Guide to the Identification of Certain American Indian Projectile Points.* Special Bulletin No. 4. Oklahoma Anthropological Society, April 1971.

Pike, Donald G., and David Muench. *Anasazi—Ancient People of the Rock* (New York: Harmony Books, A division of Crown Publishers, Inc., 1974).

Robbins, Maurice, and Mary B. Irving. *The Amateur Archaeologist's Handbook* (New York: Thomas Y. Crowell Company, 1965, 1973).

Rogers, Malcom J. *Ancient Hunters of the Far West* (San Diego, Calif.: The Union-Tribune Publishing Company, 1966).

Ronen, Avraham. *Introducing Prehistory* (London: Cassell & Company, Ltd., 1975).

Russell, Osborne. *Journal of a Trapper (1834–1843).* Edited by Aubrey L. Haines. Oregon Historical Society (Lincoln & London: University of Nebraska Press, A Bison Book Edition, 1955, 1965).

Russell, Virgil Y. *Indian Artifacts* (Boulder, Colo.: Johnson Publishing Company, 1951, 1957, 1962).

St. Vrain Valley Historical Association. *They Came to Stay* (Longmont, Colo.: St. Vrain Historical Society, Inc., 1971).

Steege, Louis C., and Warren W. Welch. *Stone Artifacts of the Northwestern Plains* (Colorado Springs, Colo.: Northwestern Plains Publishing Company, 1961).

Turner, Ellen Sue, and Thomas R. Hester. *A Field Guide to Stone Artifacts of Texas Indians* (Austin, Tex.: Texas Monthly Press, Inc., 1985).

United States Government. *Antiquities Act* (Washington, D.C.: 16 United States Code Annotated, Sections 431, 432, and 433).

United States Government. Archaeological Resources Protection Act of 1979. Washington, D.C.: 16 United States Code Annotated, Section 470, et seq. Pub. Law 96-95.

Waldorf, D. C. *The Art of Flintknapping*. 3d ed. (Branson, Mo.: Mound Builder Books, 1984).

Watson, Don. *Indians of the Mesa Verde* (Mesa Verde National Park, Colo.: Mesa Verde Museum Association, 1961).

Willey, Gordon R. *An Introduction to American Archaeology*. Vol. 1 (Englewood Cliffs, N.J.: Prentice-Hall, 1966).

Wormington, H. M. *Ancient Man in North America* (Denver, Colo.: The Denver Museum of Natural History, 1957).

Wormington, H. M., and Richard G. Forbis. *An Introduction to the Archaeology of Alberta, Canada* (Denver, Colo.: The Denver Museum of Natural History, 1965).

Yeager, C. G., ed. *History of the Stone Age Fair* (Loveland, Colo.: The Loveland Archaeological Society, Inc., 1990).

Zim, Herbert S.; Paul R. Shaffer; and Raymond Perlman. *Rocks and Minerals* (New York: Golden Press, Inc., 1957).

MEET THE AUTHOR

C. G. "Gary" Yeager, of Loveland, Colorado, has been a student of archaeology for more than forty years. He has been a practicing attorney for thirty years after serving in the United States Navy in the Vietnam War. A descendant of early Colorado settlers, Gary is proud of his agricultural heritage and his degree in Agricultural Business, which he received from Colorado State University in 1964. His grandfather cultivated his interest in archaeology by taking him arrowhead hunting in the early 1950s after his first visit to the Loveland Stone Age Fair.

Gary has been a history buff and collector of interesting items for most of his life. In addition to stone artifacts, he also collects farm toys, pencils and pens, and various other nostalgic memorabilia. He also has a strong interest in pastel artwork, which he sells regularly, and has played finger-style guitar for many years. He has had a longtime association with the Loveland Archaeological Society and has served as chairman of the annual Loveland Stone Age Fair for many years.

Despite all of his extracurricular activities, he still enjoys his family and family activities most of all. Gary and his wife, Sue, live on rural acreage in Colorado, not far from their daughter, Debbie, and her family.

Illustration 153 *Sand Creek*, Laramie Plains, one example of the author's pastel landscapes.

INDEX